The Book of American Trade Marks

Published by Century Communications Unlimited, Inc.
1500 Carter Avenue, Ashland, Ky. 41101

Edited by
David E. Carter

Century Communications Unlimited, Inc.
1500 Carter Avenue, P.O. Box 681
Ashland, Kentucky 41101

Library of Congress Catalog Card Number: 72-76493

Introduction

Some time in the late 1950s or early 1960s, a graphic revolution started. An unprecedented number of companies decided to update their corporate symbol.

There is no single answer as to what caused this revolution. Part of the reason was the great number of mergers and acquisitions in the past 10-15 years. Thousands of companies are merging every year. More often than not, the resulting company emerges with a new corporate name — and a new corporate symbol.

Another partial explanation is that, for some reason, companies became more image conscious. Corporate symbols that had been created many years before looked out of step with the times. Many companies made the decision to update their image.

This book is an attempt to show some of the significant trade marks, logotypes, and corporate symbols that now exist in the United States. The contents of this book are meant to reflect the sweeping changes which have taken place in corporate symbol design. The nearly 1,000 corporate symbols included in this book are all considered by the editor to be outstanding examples of contemporary design.

It is readily apparent that this book does not include every good corporate symbol in the United States. (There are certainly more than 992 good marks now in existence.) For this reason, and because of enthusiastic response to the idea of this book, a Volume 2 of The Book of American Trade Marks is now in the early stages of preparation.

Persons wishing to submit marks to be considered for inclusion may mail them to Century Communications Unlimited, Inc., PO Box 681, 1500 Carter Avenue, Ashland, Kentucky, 41101.

Marks will not be returned, but all material will be acknowledged.

Many of the marks included in this book are registered trade marks. and may not be reproduced without the permission of the owner of the mark.

I would like to thank the many designers and owners of trade marks who have given permission for material to be included in this book.

I would also like to give special thanks to Roger S. Dyer, who assisted in all phases of this project (which has taken more than three years), and to A.T. Turnbull of Ohio University, and to Bob McKinney and Dave Brumfield of Chapman Printing Co., for assistance in pre-press production of the book.

For my mother, who made everything possible, and for my wife, whose patience and understanding made this book possible.

1

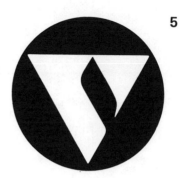

5

GATX

2

6

3

7

4

8

9

10

11

12

1 Perfection Gear Company
Chicago

2 GATX
Chicago

3 Camp Rafa-El
Marin Jewish Community Center

4 Salesvertising Art
Denver

5 Varo, Inc.
Garland, Texas

6 Redactron Corporation
Hauppauge, New York

7 Recognition Equipment, Inc.
Dallas

8 Acheson Colloids Co.
Port Huron, Michigan

9 New England Aquarium
Boston

10 United Banks of Colorado
Denver

11 White House Conference on Youth
Washington

12 Seatrain Lines
New York City

13

17

14

18

15

19

16

20

21

22

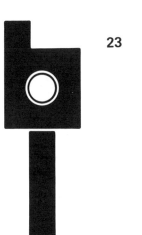

23

13 The General Fireproofing Co.
Youngstown, Ohio

14 American Revolution Bicentennial Comm.
Washington, D.C.

15 New York State University of Buffalo
Buffalo

16 Lake Forest National Bank
Lake Forest, Illinois

17 Willow Creek Apartments
Lake Forest, Illinois

18 CBS
New York City

19 Imperial International Learning
Kankakee, Illinois

20 Follett Educational Corp.
Chicago

21 Marcal Paper Mills, Inc.

22 Citizens National Bank
Bowling Green, Kentucky

23 Blakeslee-Lane Photography
Baltimore

24 Beverly Hills Tennis Club
Beverly Hills, California

24

25

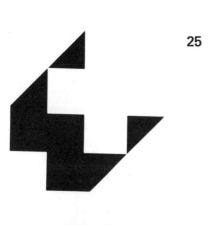

29

26

30

27

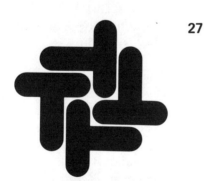

31

28

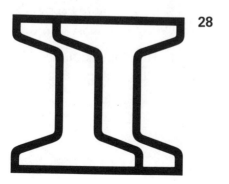

32

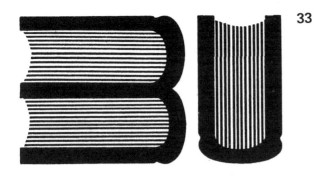

33

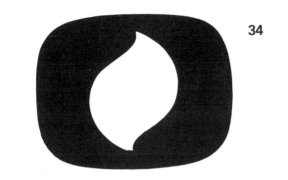

34

35

36

25 Beekman Downtown Hospital
New York City

26 Cooper Tool Co.
Denver

27 Titan Fastners
Roslyn, New York

28 Isramet Trading Corporation
Greenvale, New York

29 Howell Design Associates
Providence, Rhode Island

30 Janet Rosenblum, Inc.
New York City

31 Phili-tec Division
Western World Electronics Corp.
New York City

32 Tern Contracting Corporation
Brooklyn

33 Books Unlimited
Sarasota, Florida

34 Torrid Oven, Inc.
Buffalo, New York

35 Uniworld Export Corporation
New York City

36 Kasparians, Inc.
Los Angeles

37

FRANKLIN TOWN

41

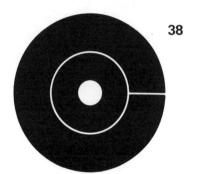

38

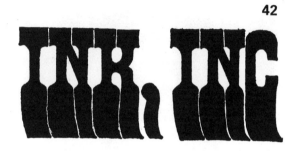

42

INK, INC

39

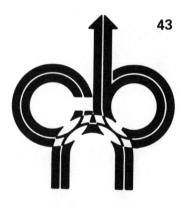

43

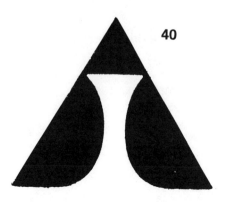

40

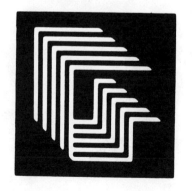

44

45

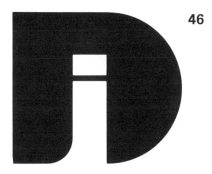

46

47

48

37 Franklin Town
Philadelphia

38 Capitol Records
Hollywood

39 Vibrodyne, Inc.
Dayton, Ohio

40 Intertechnique
Dover, New Jersey

41 Envirotech Corporation
Menlo Park, California

42 Ink, Inc.
Lakewood, Colorado

43 City National Bank
Austin, Texas

44 W.D. Gradison & Company
Cincinnati

45 Delaware Management Co., Inc.
Philadelphia

46 Decatur Income Fund
Philadelphia

47 Delta Trend Fund
Philadelphia

48 Delaware Fund
Philadelphia

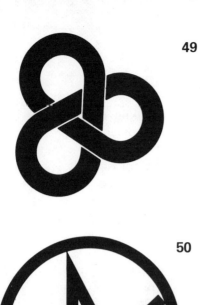 49

 53

 50

 54

51

 55

 52

56

57

58

59

60

49 MPB Corporation
Keene, New Hampshire

50 John Birdsall Creative Service Assoc.
Los Angeles

51 Marker-Berry Graphics
San Francisco

52 Gallmeyer & Livingston Co.
Grand Rapids, Michigan

53 Peace Corps
Washington

54 Canadian Waters, Inc.
Ely, Minnesota

55 Public Service Indiana
Plainfield, Indiana

56 Emhart Corporation
Hartford, Connecticut

57 Fourth National Bank
Tulsa, Oklahoma

58 The Decker Clark Corporation

59 International Minerals & Chemicals
Chicago

60 The Platt Bros. & Co.
Waterbury, Connecticut

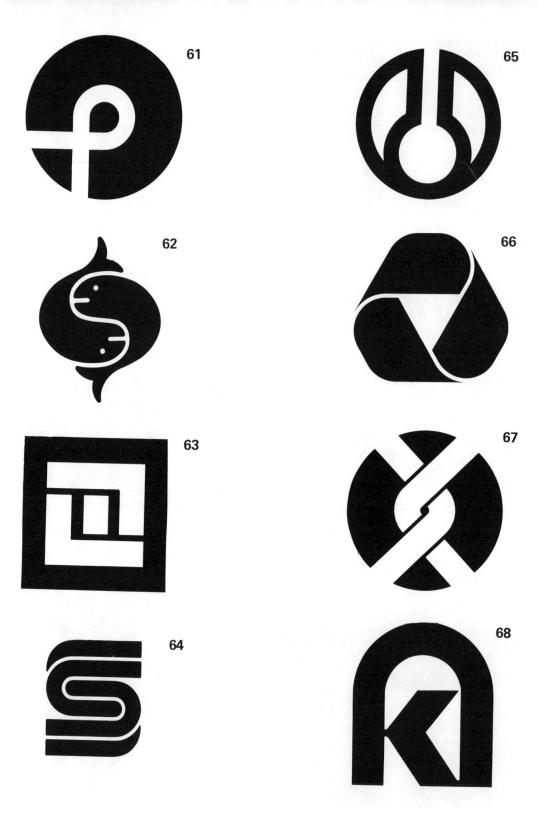

61

65

62

66

63

64

67

68

69

70

71

72

61 Pembroke's
Salt Lake City, Utah

62 Aquaria, Inc.
Los Angeles

63 Franklin Interiors
Pittsburgh

64 Security First National Bank
Los Angeles

65 International Applied Science Laboratory
Hempstead, L.I., New York

66 Innerspace Environments, Inc.
San Francisco

67 American Protection Industries
Los Angeles

68 Keepper Nagel, Inc.
Lake Forest, Illinois

69 Morris Museum of Arts & Sciences
Morristown, N. J.

70 Jim Lucas Photography
Oklahoma City, Oklahoma

71 Pacific Electrical
Gardena, California

72 View Seal
Container Corporation of America
New York City

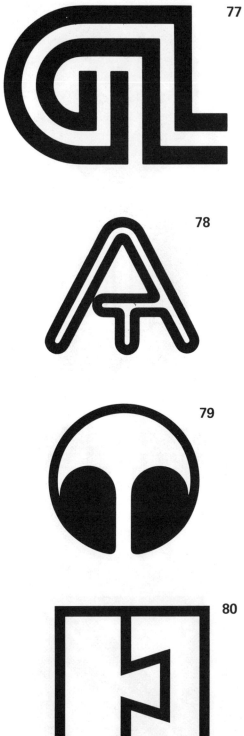

73

74

75

76

77

78

79

80

81

82

83

84

73 M.C. Canfield Sons, Quality Solder
Union, New Jersey

74 Lee Myles Assoc., Inc., Advertising
New York City

75 Lee Myles Assoc., Inc., Printing
New York City

76 Carrier Envelope Co.
Chicago

77 General Learning Corporation
New York City

78 American Tube and Controls Inc.
West Warwick, Rhode Island

79 First National Bank in Palm Beach
Palm Beach, Florida

80 Foothill General Corporation
Century City, California

81 Technical Exhibits Corporation
Subsidiary of Model Builders, Inc.
Chicago

82 Carefree Services
Denver

83 Teledyne, Inc.
Los Angeles

84 RCA
New York City

85

89

86

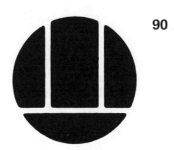
90

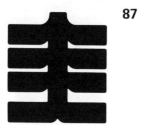
87

91

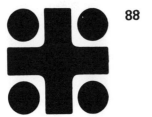
88

92

93

94

95

96

85 Penguin Industries, Inc.
   Parkesburg, Pennsylvania

86 Hoppe's, a Division of
   Penguin Industries, Inc.
   Parkesburg, Pennsylvania

87 Redwood Bank
   San Rafael, California

88 Typagraph Corporation
   San Diego, California

89 Holiday Airlines
   Los Angeles

90 Merchants Bank of Allentown
   Allentown, Pennsylvania

91 Bianco Manufacturing Co.
   St. Louis

92 United Engineers & Contractors, Inc.
   Philadelphia

93 Nor-Lake, Inc.
   Hudson, Wisconsin

94 The Larwin Group, Inc.
   Beverly Hills, California

95 Ohio National Bank
   Columbus, Ohio

96 Norman L. Mayell & Associates
   Chicago

97

101

98

102

99

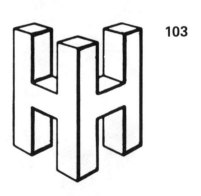

103

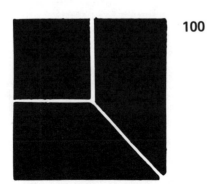

100

104

105

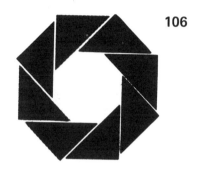

106

107

108

97 Equity Funding Corp. of America
Los Angeles

98 Air Products and Chemicals, Inc.
Allentown, Pennsylvania

99 Southern Natural Gas Co.
Birmingham, Alabama

100 College/University Corporation
Indianapolis

101 Goulds Pumps
Seneca Falls, New York

102 Buffalo Savings Bank
Buffalo, New York

103 Hartford Hospital
Hartford, Connecticut

104 Imaginetics, Inc.
White Plains, New York

105 Tropical Air Pump Mfg. Corp.
New York City

106 Color Service, Inc.
Monterey Park, California

107 Aerostar, Ted Smith
Aircraft Co., Inc.
Van Nuys, California

108 The Carborundum Co.
Niagara Falls, New York

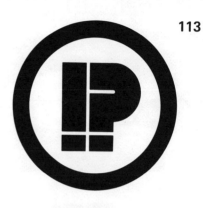

109

113

110

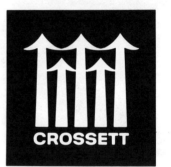

114

111

115

CROSSETT

112

116

 117

 118

 119

 120

109 Gordo Records
Los Angeles

110 Atlantic Richfield Co.
New York City

111 Ekco Products, Inc.
Wheeling, Illinois

112 The Durst Organization
New York City

113 Problematics
Waltham, Massachusetts

114 Pollota & Sommers,
General Contractors
Palisades Park, New Jersey

115 The Crossett Company
Crossett, Arkansas

116 Heatilator Fireplaces
Vega Industries
Syracuse, New York

117 Ducommun Incorporated
Los Angeles

118 Ducommun Metals & Supply Co.
Los Angeles

119 Kierulff Electronics, Inc.
Los Angeles

120 Super-Temp Co.
Santa Fe Springs, California

121

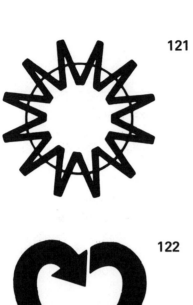

125

122

126

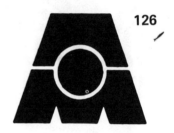

123

127

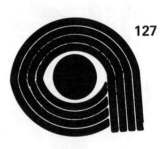

124

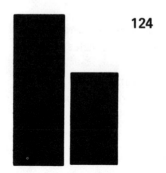

128

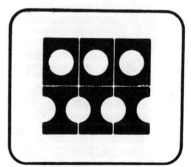

129

130

131

132

121 Sun Newspapers
   Edina, Minnesota

122 Valentine Pulp & Paper Co.
   Lockport, Louisiana

123 Jeppesen & Co.
   Denver

124 Hooker Chemical Corp.
   New York City

125 Beverly Hills Bancorp
   Beverly Hills, California

126 Ajax Magnathermatic Corp.
   Warren, Ohio

127 American Sentry Corp.
   Beverly Hills, California

128 Information International
   Los Angeles

129 Metropolitan Wire Goods Corp.
   Wilkes-Barre, Pennsylvania

130 Jacks 4
   Thousand Oaks, California

131 Aspen Skiing Corp.
   Aspen Colorado

132 Central Penn National Bank
   Philadelphia

133

137

134

138

135

139

136

140

141

142

143

144

133 Bankers Trust
New York City

134 Lawter Chemicals, Inc.
Chicago

135 Toyo Printing Co.
Los Angeles

136 Merchants Insurance Group
Buffalo, New York

137 Cascade Electric
Tacoma, Washington

138 Advance Mortgage Corp.
Southfield, Michigan

139 Johnson Foils, Inc.
Springfield, Massachusetts

140 Cascade Airways
Spokane, Washington

141 California Products Corp.
Cambridge, Massachusetts

142 Quality Cheese & Spice
Somerville, Massachusetts

143 Massachusetts Bank & Trust
Brockton, Massachusetts

144 First National Bank
Dayton, Ohio

145

149

146

150

147

151

148

152

153

154

155

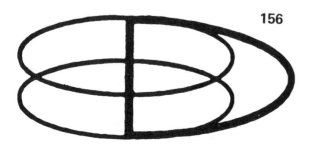

156

145 Finn Industries
Chicago

146 Federal Compress & Warehouse Co.
Memphis, Tennessee

147 Pioneer Electronics USA Corp.
Farmingdale, New York

148 Hancock-Gross
Philadelphia

149 New York Aquarium

150 Hardwood House
Rochester, New York

151 Spicer Divisions
Dana Corp.
Toledo, Ohio

152 Richmond Research Corp.
Richmond Hill, New York

153 Scientific Resources Corp.
Philadelphia

154 Porcelain Studio
San Francisco

155 The Seiberling Tire & Rubber Co.
Akron, Ohio

156 Dickenson Publishing Co., Inc.
Encino, California

157

161

158

162

159

163

160

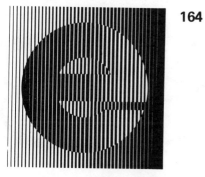

164

165

166

167

snowbird

168

157 G. Leblanc Corp.
Kenosha, Wisconsin

158 Springer-Verlag New York, Inc.
New York City

159 American Journal of Nursing
New York City

160 Loft's Candy Co.
Long Island City, New York

161 The Twentieth Century Fund
New York City

162 Bank of the Commonwealth
Norfolk, Virginia

163 Industrial Design Collaborative
Brooklyn

164 Eisert Racing Enterprises, Inc.
Costa Mesa, California

165 Rochester Institute of Technology
Rochester, New York

166 Lone Star Industries, Inc.
Greenwich, Connecticut

167 Snowbird, Ltd.
Alta, Utah

168 Northwest Bancorporation
Minneapolis

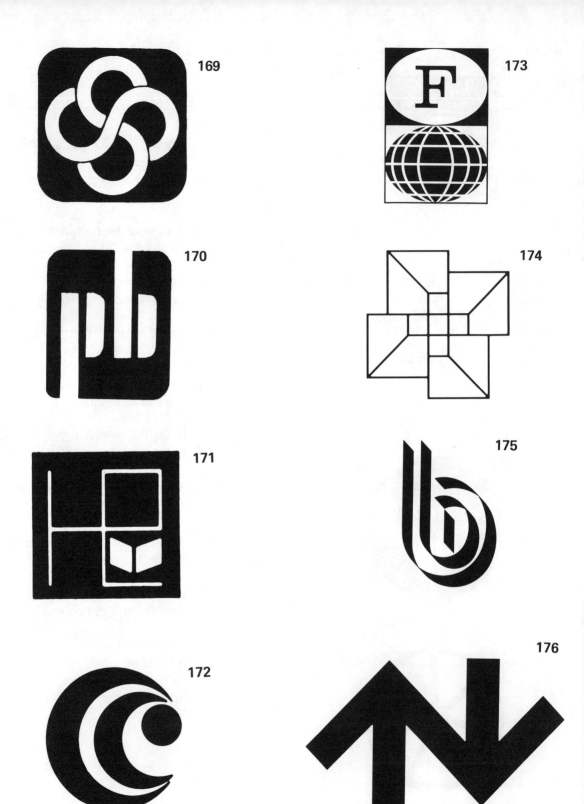

169

173

170

174

171

175

172

176

177

169 Oakley Tube Corp.
Englewood, Colorado

170 Peoples Bank of Western Pennsylvania
New Castle, Pennsylvania

171 Hartford Public Library
Hartford, Connecticut

172 Conwed Corp.
St. Paul, Minnesota

173 Follett Corporation
Chicago

174 Omniplan
Dallas

175 Brammer's Business Interiors
Memphis, Tennessee

176 National Elevator

177 American Greetings Corporation
Cleveland

178 Prudent Publishing Co.
Englewood Cliffs, New Jersey

179 Matheson Gas Products
Milwaukee

180 W.H. Freeman and Co., Publishers
San Francisco

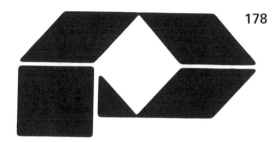

178

179

180

181

185

182

186

183

187

184

188

189

190

191

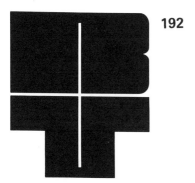

192

181 Jefferson National Bank
Lynchburg, Virginia

182 Delray Dunes Golf & Country Club
Delray Beach, Florida

183 Corpus Christi Bank & Trust
Corpus Christi, Texas

184 First National Bank
Hot Springs, Arkansas

185 Lawry's Foods, Inc.
Los Angeles

186 Photographic Display Laboratories
St. Paul, Minnesota

187 Baseler Photo Marketing Co., Inc.

188 The Continental Bank
Chicago

189 Gillette Tolitries
Boston

190 Huntly Gaming Company
Beverly Hills, California

191 Klopman Mills
New York City

192 Burns & Towne
Malden, Massachusetts

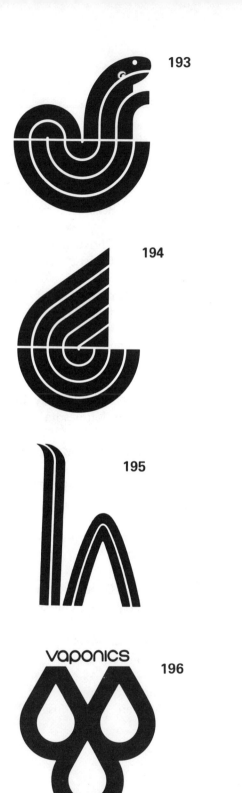

193

194

195

vaponics

196

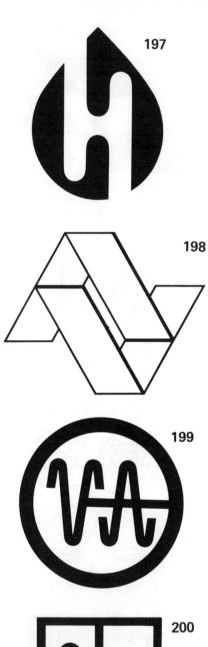

197

198

199

goodwill

200

201

202

203

204

193 Beaver Cove
Greenville, Maine

194 Beaver Cove Marina
Greenville, Maine

195 Haystack Ski Area
Vermont

196 Vaponics
Dedham, Massachusetts

197 Houghton Chemical Corp.
Boston

198 Architectural Design Assoc.
Providence, Rhode Island

199 Varian
Palo Alto, California

200 Goodwill Industries
Boston

201 Turbo Train Transportation
U.S. Dept. of Transportation
Washington

202 Martin Senour Paints
Chicago

203 Corporate Identities
Division of Gray & Rogers
Philadelphia

204 Clay-Adams
Parsippany, New Jersey

IBM
205

206

207

208

209

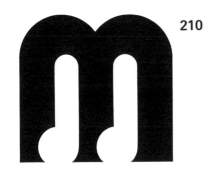

210

211

MIDDLE SOUTH
UTILITIES SYSTEM

212

205 IBM
     New York City

206 Sperry Rand Corp.
     New York City

207 Pennwalt Corp.
     Philadelphia

208 Universal Airlines
     New York City

209 Edgewood Furniture Co., Inc.
     New York City

210 Manhattan School of Music
     New York City

211 Middle South Services Inc.
     New Orleans,

212 Eidophor Inc.
     Division of CIBA

213

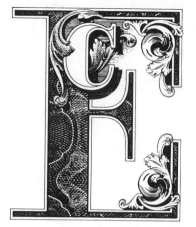

217

214

218

215

219

216

220

221

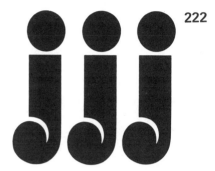

222

223

224

213 Creative Equity Corp.
     Redondo Beach, California

214 National Council of Negro Women

215 Bryant Press
     New York City

216 Scott Engineering Sciences
     Pompano Beach, Florida

217 Burlington Northern
     St. Paul, Minnesota

218 Fain's Floor Covering
     Providence, Rhode Island

219 Marine Midland Bank
     New York City

220 Montessori Family Centre
     Boston

221 Sperti Sunlamp Division
     Ft. Mitchell, Kentucky

222 Salada Foods
     Junket Dessert Tablets
     Woodburn, Massachusetts

223 Walter Kidde & Co.
     Belleville, New Jersey

224 Sundial Electronic Corp.
     Greenvale, L.I., New York

225

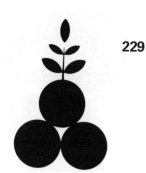

229

226

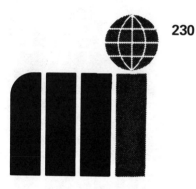

230

227

231

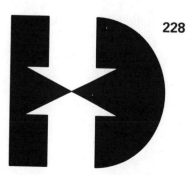

228

232

233

234

235

236

225 Philadelphia Chapter, AIA
Philadelphia

226 Allied Casting Corp.
Philadelphia

227 Erfft Associates, Inc.
Philadelphia

228 Dynastructures, Inc.
Philadelphia

229 Gettysburg Urban Renewal
Gettysburg, Pennsylvania

230 Mayfran, Inc.
Cleveland

231 Motorola, Inc.
Chicago

232 New York Life Insurance Co.
New York City

233 Citizens Fidelity Bank
Louisville

234 First National Bank of Minneapolis
Minneapolis

235 Gelman Instrument Co.
Ann Arbor, Michigan

236 Facit-Oohner, Inc.
Secaucus, New Jersey

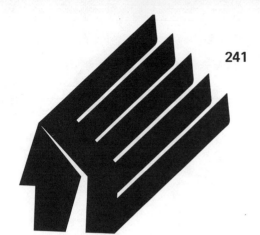

237

241

238

242

239

243

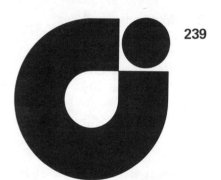

240

244

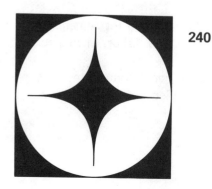

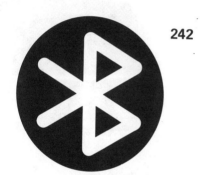

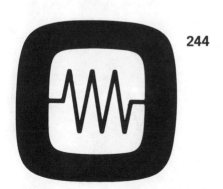

245

246

ALCAN

247

248

237 Roth Office Environments
Dayton, Ohio

238 Bell Brand Foods
Division of Sunshine Biscuits, Inc.
Los Angeles

239 Cordon International Corporation
West Los Angeles

240 The Exolon Co.
Tonawanda, New York

241 Industrious Agricolas
Calexico, California

242 Beaunit Corporation
New York City

243 Webb and Company
Richmond, Virginia

244 Ohmite Manufacturing Co.
Skokie, Illinois

245 Arapahoe Earth Movers
Englewood, Colorado

246 Alcan Corporation
Cleveland

247 Memphis Area Chamber of Commerce
Memphis, Tennessee

248 American-Exporter
New York City

249

250

251

252

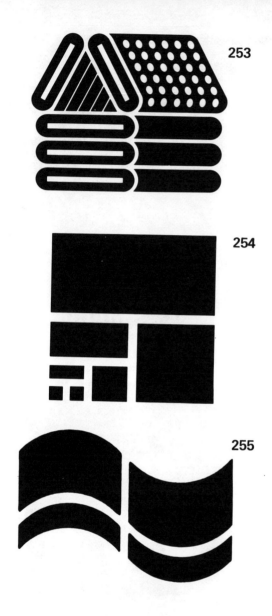

253

254

255

256

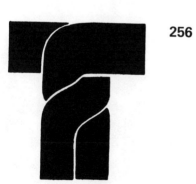

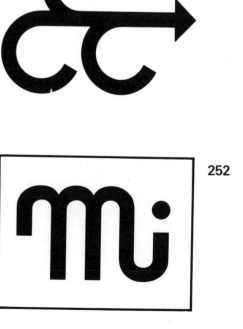

 257

 258

 259

 260

249 Florissant Land Development
Denver, Colorado

250 Rancho San Diego
San Diego

251 Corporate Communications Co., Inc.
Los Angeles

252 Marshall Industries
San Marino, California

253 House of Fabrics, Inc.
Sun Valley, California

254 The Titan Group, Inc.
Louisville, Kentucky

255 Clarksville Theatre
Clarksville, Indiana

256 Together, Inc.
Memphis, Tennessee

257 Larson Enterprises, Inc.
Los Angeles

258 Virginia Commonwealth Univ.
Richmond, Virginia

259 Tubeco Pipe Mfg. Corp.
Brooklyn

260 Triad Offset, Inc.
New York City

261

265

262

266

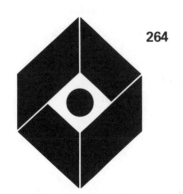

263

267

264

268

269

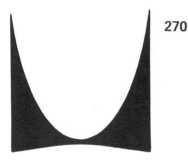

270

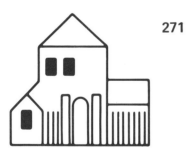

271

272

261 Beam-Cast, Inc.
Buffalo, New York

262 Malacandra Productions

263 American Republic Insurance Co.
Des Moines, Iowa

264 Main Place
Dallas

265 Community Relations Center
Boulder, Colorado

266 Hawaiian Wines, Inc.
Fresno, California

267 The Small Circle of Friends
Palo Alto, California

268 Welsh-Hannafin, Inc.
Philadelphia

269 Colorado National Bank
Denver

270 Herman Miller Inc.
Zeeland, Michigan

271 Random House
New York City

272 The Maytag Co.
Newton, Iowa

273

277

274

278

275

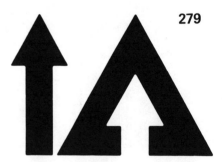

279

Arkansas

276

280

281

282

283

284

273 Architectural Pottery
Los Angeles

274 Panelgraphic Corporation
Caldwell, New Jersey

275 Aragon, International, Inc.
Boulder, Colorado

276 Arkansas Industrial Development Comm.
Little Rock

277 Brite Industries
Providence, Rhode Island

278 R & D Thiel
Palatine, Illinois

279 International Instant Archery Assn.

280 B. R. Starnes Company

281 Flex-Weld, Inc.
Bartlett, Illinois

282 Ohio Safety Systems, Inc.
Cincinnati

283 East Dayton Tool & Die Co.
Dayton, Ohio

284 Ross Yacht
Clearwater, Florida

 285

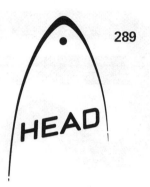 289

 286

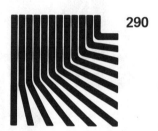 290

 287

 291

 288

 292

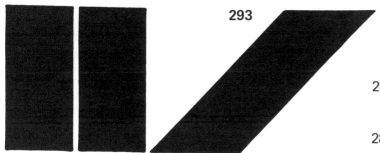

293

294

295

296

285 Parker Machine, Inc.
North Adams, Massachusetts

286 White Lines
Oxford, Ohio

287 Fuller-O'Brien Corporation
Menlo Park, California

288 Inter-Faith Task Force
Littleton, Colorado

289 Head Ski Co., Inc.
Timonium, Maryland

290 Logistics Systems, Inc.
Cambridge, Massachusetts

291 The Graphics Studio
Los Angeles

292 Weinschel Engineering
Gaithersburg, Maryland

293 Four-Phase Systems, Inc.
Cupertine, California

294 Sherer-Gillett Co.
Marshall, Michigan

295 Applied Logic Corp.

296 Lord & Burnham
Irvington-on-Hudson, New York

297

301

298

302

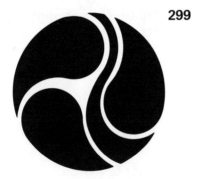

299

303

300

304

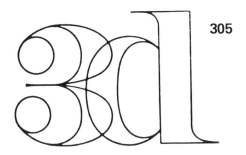

305

306

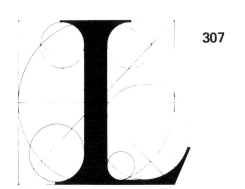

307

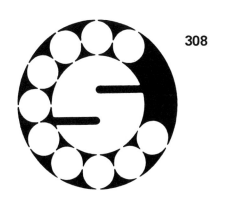

308

297 Brown-Foreman Distillers Corp.
Louisville, Kentucky

298 Philadelphia Diagnostic & Rehabilitation Serv.
Philadelphia

299 Pennsylvania, New Jersey & Delaware
Committee of Governors
Philadelphia

300 Lutheran Fraternal Organizations
Appleton, Wisconsin

301 South Carolina National Bank
Columbia, South Carolina

302 Stop and Shop
Boston

303 Medi Mart
Bosotn

304 Fun Stop
Boston

305 Third Dimension Studio
Wichita, Kansas

306 Asgrow Seed Company
Orange, Connecticut

307 Letterforms
New York City

308 Sterling Answer Service
Wilton, Connecticut

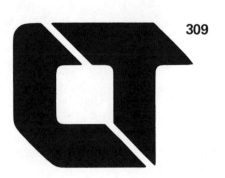
309

313

310

314

311

315

312

316

317

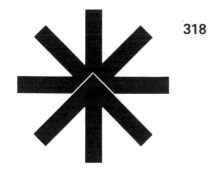

318

319

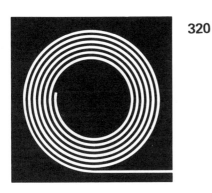

320

309 Cleveland Trust
Cleveland, Ohio

310 North American Rockwell
Pittsburgh

311 Charles Schnier Development Co.
Bloomfield, Connecticut

312 Gravely Corporation
Clemmons, North Carolina

313 The Aluminum Association
New York City

314 Agricultural Missions, Inc.
New York City

315 Broward Bancshares, Inc.
Ft. Lauderdale, Florida

316 Makaha Inn
Waianae, Oahu, Hawaii

317 Boles Aero, Inc.
Sun Valley, California

318 Merchandise Display, Inc.
Dayton, Ohio

319 Cleveland Institute of Art
Cleveland

320 Washington Steel Co.
Washington, Pennsylvania

321

325

322

326

323

327

324

328

U.S. DEPARTMENT OF THE INTERIOR

329

330

331

332

321 Associated Spring Co.
Briston, Connecticut

322 New York School of Interior Design
New York City

323 Helbros Watches
New York City

324 Western International Hotels
Seattle, Washington

325 SMC Industries, Inc.
Chattanooga, Tennessee

326 Swedcast Division
Swedlow, Inc.
Florence, Kentucky

327 American International Bank
New York City

328 U.S. Department of the Interior
Washington, D. C.

329 Medalist Industries
Milwaukee

330 Carlton Screw Mfg. Co.
Northfield, Illinois

331 Graphic Communications
Little Rock, Arkansas

332 Laco Signs, Inc.
Libertyville, Illinois

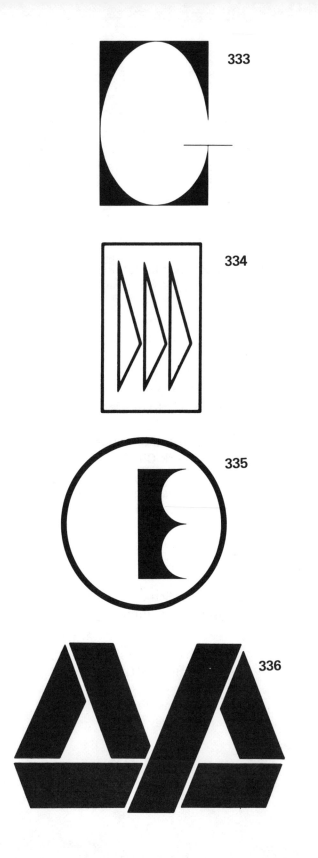

333

334

335

336

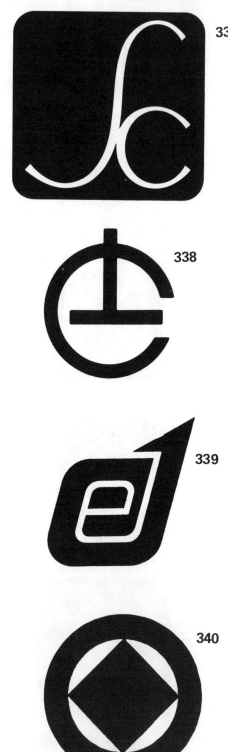

337

338

339

340

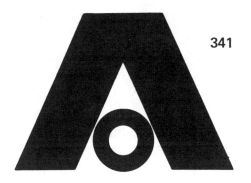

341

342

343

344

333 Poultry Guild
Moorefield, West Virginia

334 Planning Research

335 The Barden Corporation
Danbury, Connecticut

336 Moore Business Forms
Niagara Falls, New York

337 Sculpture Collectors, Ltd.
New York City

338 J.L. Clark
Rockford, Illinois

339 Economic Development Corp. of
San Diego County

340 Bronwill Scientific Inc.
Rochester, New York

341 American Cast Iron Pipe Co.
Birmingham, Alabama

342 Hankscraft
Reedsburg, Wisconsin

343 Behlen Mfg. Co.
Columbus, Nebraska

344 Land Search Corporation
Seattle, Washington

345

346

boren's

347

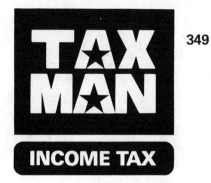

349

INCOME TAX

350

351

348

New England Farms

352

house of ronnie, inc

353

354

355

KENDALL

356

345 Bay State Abrasives

346 Goren Foods Co.
Boston

347 William J. Burns Detective Agency

348 New England Farms
Arlington, Massachusetts

349 Tax Man
Cambridge, Massachusetts

350 Sunnyside Products, Inc.
Chicago

351 C.A. Norgren Co.
Littleton, Colorado

352 House of Ronnie, Inc.
New York City

353 EG&G
Bedford, Massachusetts

354 Anzio (movie)

355 The Kendall Co.
New York City

356 Living Marine Resources, Inc.
San Diego

 357

 361

Mister Donut

 358

 362

 359

 363

 360

 364

365

366

367

368

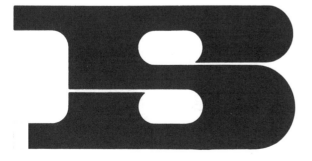

357 Presbyterian Hospital Center
    Albuquerque, New Mexico

358 Mountain Sports
    Boulder, Colorado

359 Ajax Hardware Corp.
    City of Industry, California

360 Strathmore Paper Co.
    West Springfield, Massachusetts

361 Mister Donut
    Westwood, Massachusetts

362 United Bank & Trust Co.
    Hartford, Connecticut

363 Willamette Industries, Inc.
    Albany, Oregon

364 Nancy Martin Public Relations
    Los Angeles

365 Maine Savings Bank
    Portland, Maine

366 Aero Bankers
    Denver, Colorado

367 LaChoy Food Products
    Div. of Beatrice Foods Co.

368 Brennan & Sloane Construction Co.

369

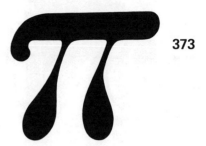

373

370

374

371

375

372

376

377

378

379

380

369 Culligan, Inc.
Northbrook, Illinois

370 Central Soya
Ft. Wayne, Indiana

371 MIT Press
Cambridge, Massachusetts

372 Foster Parents Plan, Inc.
New York City

373 Pyttronic Inc.
Harrisburg, Pennsylvania

374 Applied Power Industries, Inc.
Milwaukee

375 Computer Products
Ft. Lauderdale, Florida

376 NBC
New York City

377 Royal Continental Box Co.
Chicago

378 Diamond Shamrock Corp.
Cleveland

379 Universal Ultrasonics, Inc.
West Babylon, New York

380 Edmund Scientific Co.
Barrington, New York

 381

 385

 382

 386

 383

 387

 384

388

389

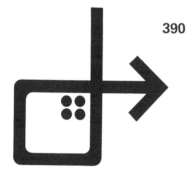

390

391

392

381 American Bankers Association

382 First National Bank in Little Rock
Little Rock, Arkansas

383 Synthane-Taylor Corporation
Valley Forge, Pennsylvania

384 Thompson-Brown Co.

385 World Airways Inc.
Oakland, California

386 The National Bank
St. Petersburg, Florida

387 Bank of Commerce
Milwaukee

388 Ingram Paper Co.
Los Angeles

389 Speekrack, Inc.
Skokie, Illinois

390 Dukane Press
Hollywood, Florida

391 Velsicol Chemical Corp.
Chicago

392 Deere & Company
Moline, Illinois

393

397

394

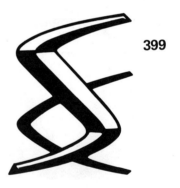

398

395

399

396

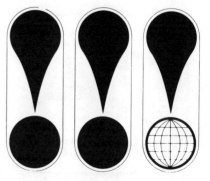

400

401

402

403

404

393 Computer Knowledge Corp.
San Antonio, Texas

394 Clevepak Corp.
New York City

395 Piedmont Minerals Company, Inc.
Greensboro, North Carolina

396 Directional Industries, Inc.
New York City

397 American Institute of Architects
New York City

398 Albright-Knox Art Gallery
Buffalo, New York

399 Superior Coach Corp.
Lima, Ohio

400 LaBow, Haynes Co., Inc.
Seattle, Washington

401 Boothe Resources International, Inc.
Los Angeles

402 Stow-Davis Furniture Co.
Grand Rapids, Michigan

403 Madison Square Garden
New York City

404 Pacific Palm Pools
Latham, New York

405

409

406

410

407

411

408

412

413

414

415

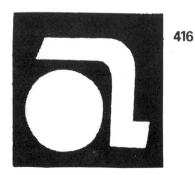

416

405 Moen, a Division of
     Stanadyne
     Elyria, Ohio

406 Foster's Meats
     Manchester, New Hampshire

407 Cameron Machine Co.
     Dover, New Jersey

408 Sawyer Industries, Inc.
     Arcadia, California

409 Halliday & Blalock, Inc.
     Louisville, Kentucky

410 Insurance Company of North America
     Philadelphia

411 United Yarn Products Co., Inc.
     Paterson, New Jersey

412 Pellon Corp.
     New York City

413 Charles Industries
     Upper Montclair, New Jersey

414 Diehl Pumps Co.
     Louisville, Kentucky

415 Self Development, Inc.
     San Jose, California

416 Amplex Mfg. Co.
     Philadelphia

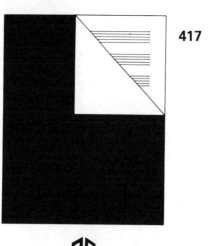 417

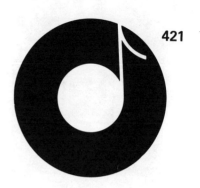 421

 418

 422

 419

 423

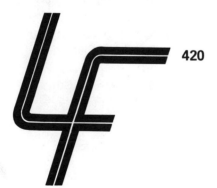 420

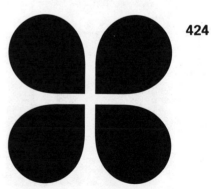 424

 **425**

 **426**

 **427**

 **428**

417 Screen Gems — Columbia Publications

418 Mount Attitash Association
     North Conway, New Hampshire

419 NYU Glee Club
     New York City

420 Lauter-Franklin Road Paving
     Flatwoods, Kentucky

421 Screen Gems — Columbia Music
     New York City

422 Greater Washington Jewish Community Fndn.
     Washington, D.C.

423 Girard Bank
     Philadelphia

424 J.F. Freeman, Inc.
     Los Angeles

425 Maico Hearing Instruments
     Minneapolis

426 Northwestern National Life Insurance Co.
     Minneapolis

427 Vance, Sanders & Co., Inc.
     Boston

428 Form & Function
     Philadelphia

 429

 433

 430

 434

 431

 435

 432

 436

437

438

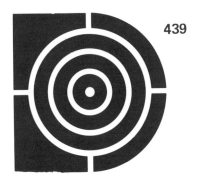

439

440

429 Time Equities Corp.
New York City

430 Newport Center
Newport Beach, California

431 Grayrock Oil & Gas
Dallas

432 Franklin Supply Co.
Denver

433 Government in the Modern World
Macmillan Company
New York City

434 Scubapro Diving Equipment
Los Angeles

435 Polyplan Plastic Products Mfg.
Santa Barbara, California

436 Southern Cross Industries, Inc.
Atlanta

437 First National Bank
Memphis, Tennessee

438 Aircraft Radio Corp.
Boonton, New Jersey

439 The Charles Stark Draper
Laboratory of MIT
Cambridge, Massachusetts

440 Watkins-Johnson Co.
Palo Alto, California

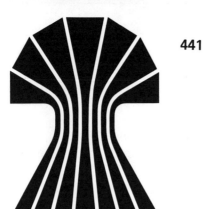

441

445

442

446

443

sun and powder

447

444

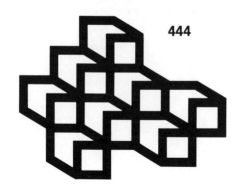

448

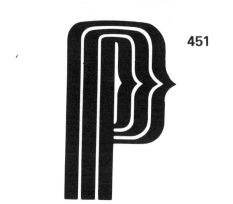

441 Comerco, Inc.
Tacoma, Washington

442 Pacific National Bank of Washington

443 Sun and Powder, Inc.
Sun Valley, Idaho

444 The Community Banks of Washington

445 The American Forest Institute
Washington, D.C.

446 Great Northwest Federal Savings & Loan Assn.

447 Arthur Cox & Sons, Inc.
Pasadena, California

448 Fremerman-Papin, Inc.
Kansas City, Missouri

449 Bell Records
New York City

450 Schorr Brothers
Brooklyn

451 People's Bank
Providence, Rhode Island

452 Hennessey Three Star Industries
Los Angeles

453

457

454

458

455

459

456

460

 **461**

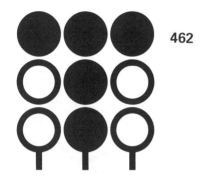 **462**

 **463**

 **464**

453   War/Peace Report, Inc.
New York City

454   Unifair, Inc.
New York City

455   Patient Care Projects Division
Miller & Fink Publishers
Greenwich, Connecticut

456   Innovation House, Inc.
New York City

457   Growth Fund of America, Inc.
Greenwich, Connecticut

458   Income Fund of America, Inc.
Greenwich, Connecticut

459   Farmlands U.S.A.
New Jersey

460   Recreation Industries, Inc.
Los Angeles

461   Data Network Corporation
New York City

462   The Treecrop Company
Oakland

463   Berley Industries, Inc.
Brooklyn

464   The Capital Group, Inc.
Los Angeles

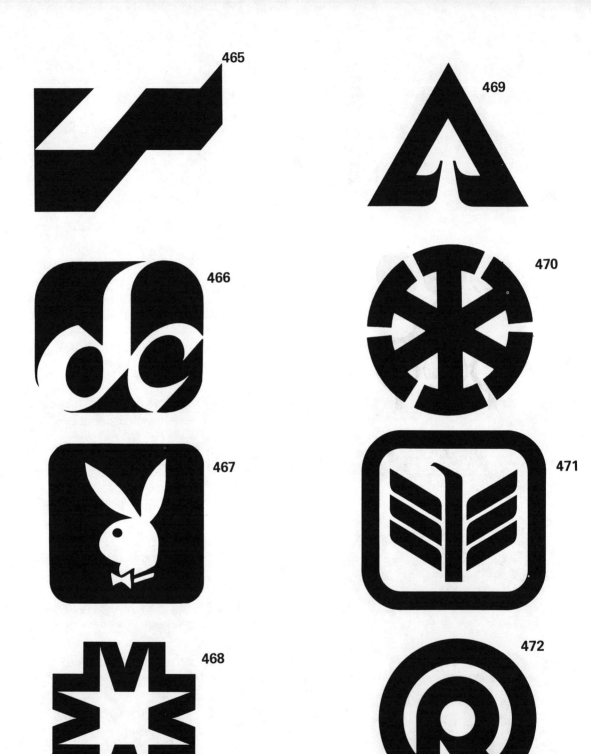

465

469

466

470

467

471

468

472

 473

 474

 475

 476

465 Tyler Pipe
subsidiary of Tyler Corporation
Tyler, Texas

466 Dodge Cork Co.
Lancaster, Pennsylvania

467 HMH Publishing Co.
Chicago

468 Metropolitan Life Insurance Co.
New York City

469 Weyerhaeuser Corporation
Tacoma, Washington

470 Temple Industries
Diboll, Texas

471 Capital National Corporation
Houston

472 Reeves Telecom Corporation
New York City

473 Hoffman-Taff, Inc.
Springfield, Mo.

474 Surety Savings & Loan Association
Burbank, California

475 International Paper Co.
New York City

476 General Oceanography
Cambridge, Massachusetts

477

481

478

479

482

483

480

484

485

486

487

488

477 Coherent Radiation Laboratories
Palo Alto, California

478 Environmental Measurements, Inc.
San Francisco

479 Marine World
Redwood City, California

480 Aerojet Liquid Rocket Company
Sacramento, California

481 Salem Plaza
Salem, Oregon

482 Lassen Volcanic National Park
Menlo Park, California

483 Mount McKinley National Park
Menlo Park, California

484 Yosemite Park and Curry Co.
Yosemite National Park, Calif.

485 Educreative Systems, Inc.
New York City

486 Citizens Federal Savings & Loan Assn.
Pittsburgh

487 Penn's Southwest Association
Pittsburgh

488 Carteret Savings & Loan Association
Newark, New Jersey

489

490

491

492

493

494

495

496

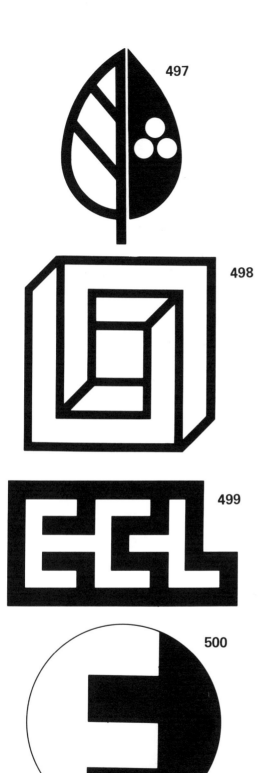

497

498

499

500

489 Security Corporation
Santa Ana, California

490 Hawaii Production Center
Honolulu

491 Cousins Properties, Inc.
Atlanta

492 Quillayote Camp
Olympic Peninsula, Washington

493 Nuclear Pacific, Inc.

494 National Forest Products Association
Washington, D. C.

495 Pepsi Cola International
Purchase, N.Y.

496 Pressman Corp. (toy manufacturers)
New York City

497 (insecticide product mark)
Upjohn Company
Kalamazoo, Michigan

498 Perfect Film & Chemical
New York City

499 ECL Industries
New York City

500 Franklin Typographers
New York City

 501

 505

 502

 502

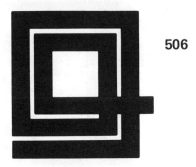 506

 503

 507

wagner

504

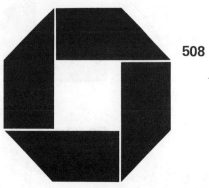 508

509

510

511

512

501   Bangor Punta Corporation
Greenwich, Connecticut

502   Milwaukee Faucets, Inc.
Milwaukee

503   Westinghouse Broadcasting Company
New York City

504   Kentucky Electric Steel Company
Ashland, Kentucky

505   WPIX Television
New York City

506   Olivetti Underwood Corporation
New York City

507   Wagner Industries, Inc.
Cicero, Illinois

508   The Chase Manhattan Bank
New York City

509   Tab
Coca-Cola Company
Atlanta

510   Armour-Dial, Inc.
Chicago

511   Kimberly-Clark Corp.
Neenah, Wisconsin

512   Comlab, Inc.
Chicago

513

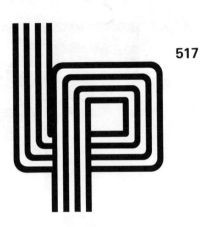

517

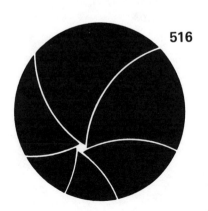

514

518

515

519

516

520

521

522

523

524

513   The Academy of Art College
San Francisco

514   Sonoco Products Co.
Hartsville, South Carolina

515   First National Bank
Baltimore

516   Omnibus Film Productions
Akron, Ohio

517   Burks Pumps
Decatur, Illinois

518   R.J. Reynolds Industries
Winston-Salem

519   Colt Industries
New York City

520   Precision Plating Co.
Chicago

521   Grossman Publishers
New York City

522   Unit 1
Denver

523
National Railroad Passenger Corp.
Washington, D.C.

524
Ex-Cell-O Corporation
Detriot

525

529

526

530

527

531

528

532

533

534

535

536

525   Spectra-Physics
Mountain View, California

526   Boise Cascade Corporation
Boise, Idaho

527   Sutro & Co., Inc.
San Francisco

528   U.S. Air Force Documentary
Art Program
Washington, D.C.

529   California Casualty Insurance Group
San Mateo, California

530   Westel Company
San Mateo, California

531   Squaw Valley Land and Livestock Co.
Tahoe City, California

532   Hagemeister-Lert, Inc.
San Francisco,

533   Tahoe Keys
Tahoe Valley, California

534   Crystal Shores
Crystal Bay, Nevada

535   The Red Radish (restaurant)
Olympic Valley, California

536   Committee of Arts and Lectures
University of California
Santa Cruz, California

537

541

538

542

539

543

540

544

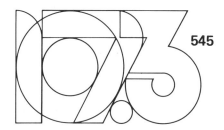

545

546

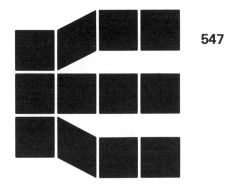

547

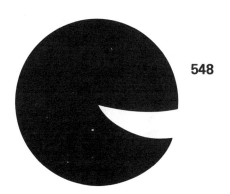

548

537 Montague-Spragens Printers
     Berkeley, California

538 Nytron, Inc.
     Palo Alto, California

539 Barr Chemical Products, Inc.
     Berkeley, California

540 Pace Fund
     Stanford University
     Stanford, California

541 Consumer Alliance
     Palo Alto, California

542 Patchcord Productions, Inc.
     Beverly Hills, California

543 WMAL TV
     Washington, D. C.

544 WCIV Television
     Mount Pleasant, S.C.

545 WMAL FM
     Washington, D.C.

546 The San Francisco Experience
     Electrovision Productions, Inc.
     San Francisco

547 Electrovision Productions, Inc.
     San Francisco

548 Cornnuts, Inc.
     Oakland, California

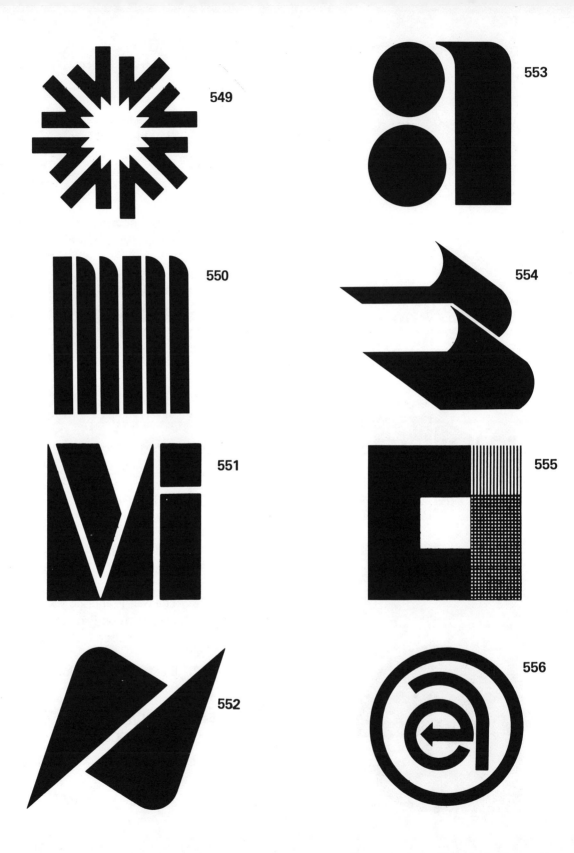

549

553

550

554

551

555

552

556

557

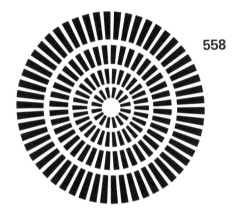

558

559

560

549 Duquesne Light
     Pittsburgh

550 Majors & Majors Realtors
     Dallas

551 Monogram Industries, Inc.
     Los Angeles

552 Nalco Chemical Co.
     Chicago

553 The Ansul Company
     Marinette, Wisconsin

554 Bellarmine College
     Louisville

555 Contract Interiors, Inc.
     Chicago

556 Aerotron, Inc.
     Raleigh

557 Signetics Corporation
     Sunnyvale, California

558 First National Bank
     Miami

559 Equitable Trust Bank
     Baltimore

560 Koracorp Industries
     San Francisco

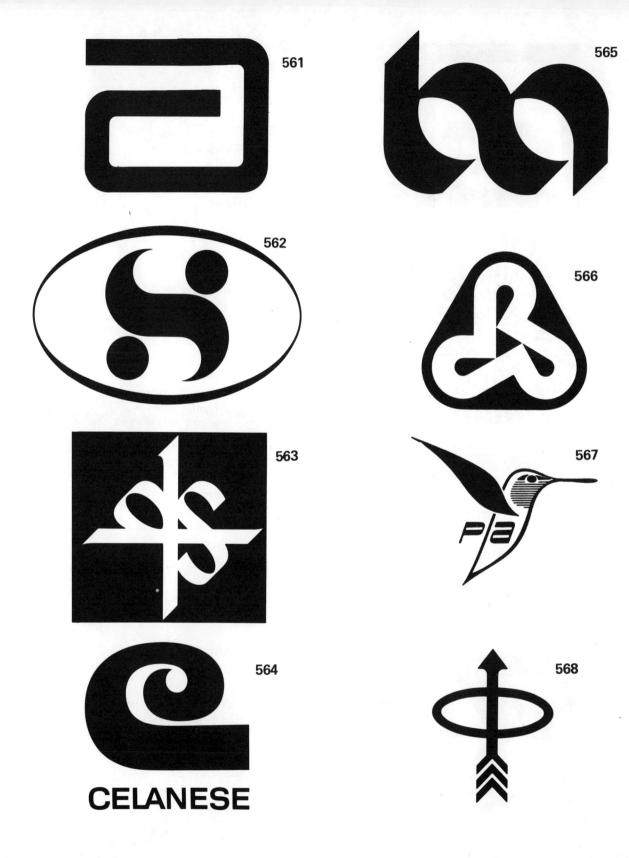

561

565

562

566

563

566

567

564

CELANESE

568

569

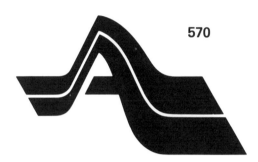

570

571

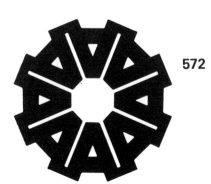

572

561 Abbott Laboratories
North Chicago, Ill.

562 Scott Paper Company
Philadelphia

563 Dayton Typographic Service
Dayton

564 Celanese Corporation
New York City

565 Bank Marketing Association
Chicago

566 Royal Industries
Pasadena

567 Pittsburgh Airways, Inc.
Pittsburgh

568 Parker Pen Co.
Janesville, Wisconsin

569 Direct Mail Advertising Assn.
New York City

570 Atlas Van Lines
Evansville, Indiana

571 Waters Associates
Framingham, Massachusetts

572 American National Bank & Trust
Chattanooga

573

577

574

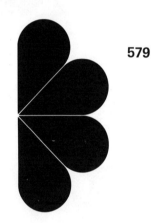
578

575

579

576

580

Mead Johnson 581
LABORATORIES

Kirsch 582

Republicsteel 583

Abex 584

573   Rose Engineering Company
      Los Angeles

574   L.J. Globus Advertising, Inc.
      Los Angeles

575   Propinquity
      Los Angeles

576   Rohm and Haas Company
      Philadelphia

577   Keller Williams Furniture Mfg. Co.
      Oklahoma City

578   Edinger-Wyckoff, Inc.
      Stroudsburg, Pennsylvania

579   Kovler Gallery
      Chicago

580   Higgins Hegner Genovese, Inc.
      Chicago

581   Mead Johnson Laboratories
      Evansville, Indiana

582   The Kirsch Company
      Sturgis, Michigan

583   Republic Steel Corporation
      Cleveland

584   Abex Corporation
      New York City

 585

 589

 586

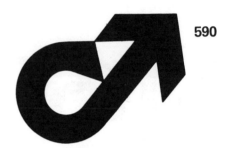 590

 587

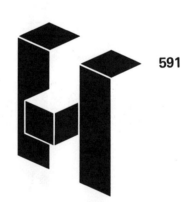 591

 588

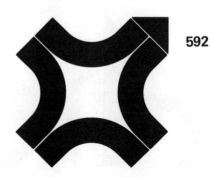 592

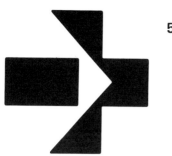 593

 594

 595

585 Bank Printing Co., Inc.
Los Angeles

586 Travenol Laboratories, Inc.
Morton Grove, Illinois

587 International Geomarine Corp.
Los Angeles

588 Aerospace Corporation
Los Angeles

589 Hospicare, Inc.
Los Angeles

590 Ohio Trailways
Oxford, Ohio

591 National Corp. for Housing
Partnerships
Washington, D. C.

592 Northeast Subway Extension
Philadelphia

593 Gould, Inc.
Chicago

594 National Energy Systems Corp.
San Francisco

595 Nashua Corp.
Nashua, New Hampshire

596 Metals Research Instrument Corp.

 596

597

601

598

602

599

603

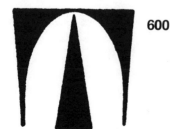
600

604

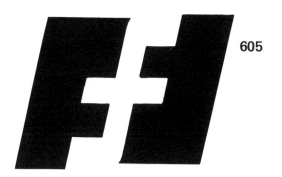 605

 606

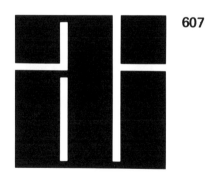 607

 608

597 Dayton Hudson Corp.
Minneapolis

598 U.S. Leasing Realty Advisers, Inc.
San Francisco

599 GAC Corporation

600 Timber Structures, Inc.
Portland, Oregon

601 Diversey Corporation
Chicago

602 Bird Precision Jewels
Waltham, Massachusetts

603 Erica Wilson, Inc.
New York City

604 Evers Savings Association
Cincinnati

605 Foremost Lithograph
Providence, Rhode Island

606 Color Concentrate Corp.
Woonsocket, Rhode Island

607 Arkwright-Interlaken, Inc.
Fiskeville, Rhode Island

608 Virginia National Bank
Norfolk, Virginia

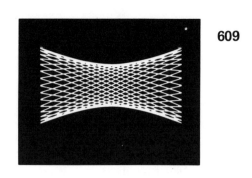

609

613

LaSalle
Steel

610

614

611

615

Wechsler

612

616

 617

 618

619

620

609 Bauer & Black
Chicago

610 LaSalle Steel

611 Bank of Maine
Augusta

612 Weschsler Coffee Corp.
New York City

613 Jeffries Banknote Co.
Los Angeles

614 Bank of the Commonwealth
Detroit

615 Steel Service Center Institute
Cleveland

616 Logan Clay`Products
Logan, Ohio

617 The Pathfinder Fund
Boston

618 Crown Paper
Yonkers, New York

619 Nuclear Data Inc.
Palatine, Illinois

620 Ditto Inc.
Lincolnwood, Illinois

621

622

623

624

625

626

627

628

621 Helipot Division
Beckman Instruments
Fullerton, California

622 Marine Sciences
Los Angeles

623 Utica Duxbax Corp.
Utica, New York

624 Goodall Rubber Co.

625 United Refining Co.
Warren, Pennsylvania

626 North American Van Lines
Ft. Wayne, Indiana

627 Keuffel & Esser Co.
Morristown, New Jersey

628 Children's Press
Chicago

629

633

630

634

631

NATIONAL CENTRAL BANK

635

632

636

637

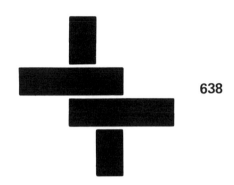

638

639

640

629 National Bank of Commerce
San Antonio

630 The Wool Bureau, Inc.
New York City

631 National Central Bank
Lancaster, Pennsylvania

632 Alpine State Bank
Rockford, Illinois

633 Ford Wire Products
Indianapolis, Indiana

634 Gate City Steel
Omaha, Nebraska

635 Universal Development Corp.
Chicago

636 KSTP Television
St. Paul, Minnesota

637 Norstar Sales Inc.
Minneapolis, Minnesota

638 Seven Lakes
Tampa, Florida

639 The Nilsen Group
Philadelphia

640 T.C. Miller Realty Co.
Akron, Ohio

 641

 645

 642

 646

 643

647

 644

648

649

650

651

652

641 United Management Services, Inc.
Houston

642 Cheyenne Mountain Ranch
Colorado Springs, Colorado

643 Eastern Stainless Steel Co.
Baltimore, Maryland

644 Screen Gems
New York City

645 Glass Containers Corporation
Fullerton, California

646 Pacific Fashion Institute
San Francisco

647 Union Planters National Bank
Memphis, Tennessee

648 Berven Carpets Corp.
Fresno, California

649 Merrill Manufacturing Corp.
Merrill, Wisconsin

650 Shelby Williams Industries, Inc.
Chicago

651 Midland Mortgage Co.
Oklahoma City, Oklahoma

652 The Lummus Co.
Bloomfield, New Jersey

 653

 657

 654

 658

655

659

 656

 660

661

662

663

664

653 Midland-Ross Corporation
Cleveland

654 Acushnet Company
New Bedford, Massachusetts

655 Western New York Savings Bank
Buffalo, New York

656 Consolidated International Corp.
Chicago

657 Diversified Products Co.
Opelika, Alabama

658 Sid Gelpe & Associates
Landscape Designers
Tarzana, California

659 Texas Gas Transmission Co.
Owensboro, Kentucky

660 Mutron
Brockton, Massachusetts

661 The Ohio Brass Co.
Mansfield, Ohio

662 A.J. Nystrom & Co.
Chicago

663 Oxford Papers
New York City

664 Multiples, Inc.
New York City

 665

 669

 666

 670

 667

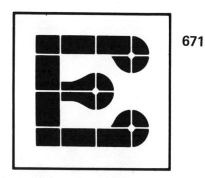 671

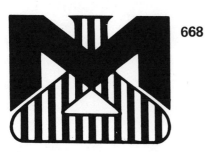 668

 672

 673

 674

 675

 676

665 Vision Craft Ltd.
Fayetteville, New York

666 The Bunker-Ramo Corp.

667 D.G. Mountz Associates, Inc.
San Jose, California

668 Matheson Scientific
Chicago

669 Standard & Poors/InterCapital, Inc.
New York City

670 Arlen Realty & Development Corp.
New York City

671 Excellon Industries
Torrance, California

672 Hitchiner Mfg. Co., Inc.
Milford, New Hampshire

673 Everbrite Electric Signs, Inc.
South Milwaukee, Wisconsin

674 Continental Steel Corp.
Kokomo, Indiana

675 Antilles Yachting Service
St. Thomas, U.S. Virgin Islands

676 Family Funding, Inc.
Cambridge, Massachusetts

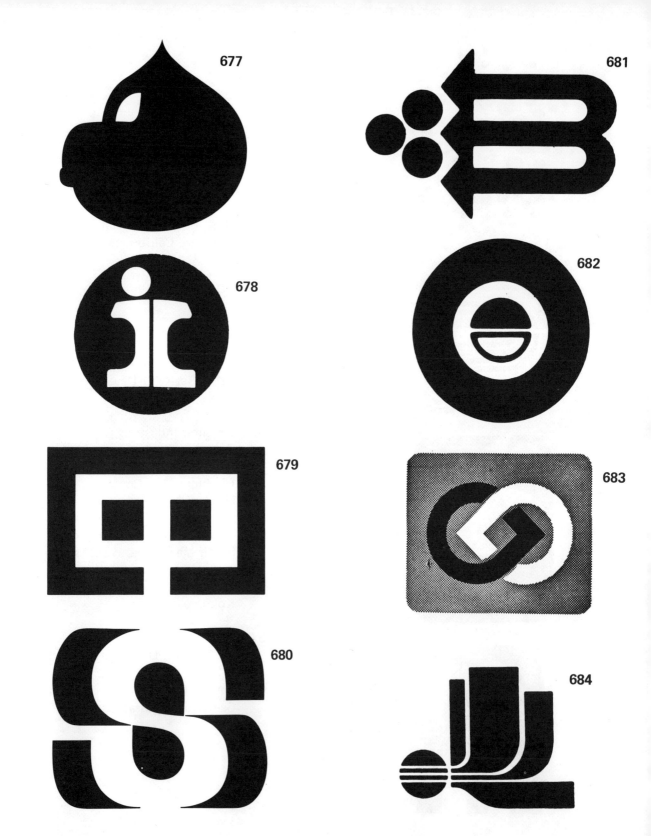

677

681

678

682

679

683

680

684

685

686

687

688

677 Hollywood Car Wash
Hollywood, California

678 Illinois Central Railroad
Chicago

679 Creative Packaging
Indianapolis

680 Southland Corporation
Dallas

681 Berg Hayslette Dupar, Inc.

682 Federal-Mogul
Detroit

683 The Bankers Life
Des Moines, Iowa

684 Realty Systems, Inc.
Denver, Colorado

685 Shultzy's
Boston

686 Delaware River Port Authority
Camden, New Jersey

687 Weltz Ad Service, Inc.
New York City

688 Ward Nassee Art Gallery
Boston

 689

 693

 690

694

 691

695

692

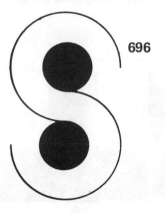 696

697

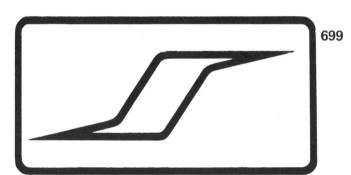

698

699

700

689 Directions or Dilemmas
Aspen, Colorado

690 American Film Institute
Washington, D.C.

691 Gottesman Central National Corp.
New York City

692 Knapp Bros. Shoe Manufacturers
Brockton, Massachusetts

693 Renauld International Ltd.
Fitchburg, Massachusetts

694 M.H.&W.
Englewood Cliffs, New Jersey

695 Jalart House
Port Chester, New Jersey

696 Suburban Printers

697 Modular Building
Benicia, California

698 Colonie Center
Albany, New York

699 Scintrex, Inc.
Tonawanda, New York

700 J.I. Case Co.
Racine, Wisconsin

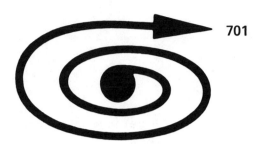 701

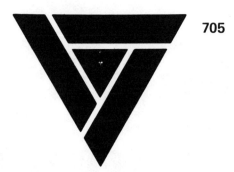 705

 702

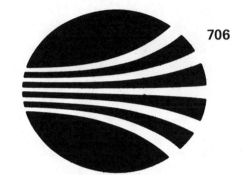 706

 703

707

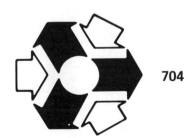 704

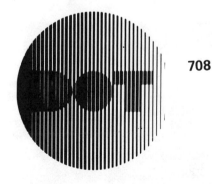 708

709

710

711

712

701 Genesco
New York City

702 Chrysler Corporation
Detroit

703 Anderson Corporation
Worcester, Massachusetts

704 McKesson & Robbins Drug Co.
New York City

705 Pittsburgh National Bank
Pittsburgh

706 Continental Airlines
Los Angeles

707 Pet, Inc.
St. Louis

708 Dot Records
Los Angeles

709 Gates Aviation Corp.
Denver

710 Joseph Love & Co.
New York City

711 American Building Maintenance Industries
San Francisco

712 DiGiorgio Development Corp.
San Francisco

713

717

714

718

715

MASTER

719

716

720

721

Cone

722

723

western union

724

ANIXTER

Bros., Inc.

713 Bank of America
     San Francisco

714 Washington Mutual Savings Bank
     Seattle, Washington

715 Master Lock Co.
     Milwaukee, Wisconsin

716 Aluminum Corp. of America
     Pittsburgh

717 School of Visual Arts
     New York City

718 Southwest Forest Industries
     Phoenix, Arizona

719 Scintillonics
     Fort Collins, Colorado

720 Atlantic National Bank
     Norfolk, Virginia

721 Cone Mills Marketing Co.
     New York City

722 Kallir, Phillips, Ross, Inc.

723 Western Union
     New York City

724 Anixter Bros., Inc.
     Skokie, Illinois

725

BRAZOS
GRAPHICS

726

729

727

730

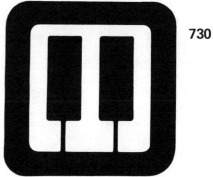

728

731

732

733

734

735

736

725 Brazos Graphics
Bryan, Texas

726 Spring '71 Bookfair
New York City

727 Trust Company Bank
Atlanta, Georgia

728 Windecker Research, Inc.
Midland, Texas

729 Art's Photo
Los Angeles

730 Magnus Organ Corporation
Linden, New Jersey

731 "Additive A"
Kimberly Clark
Neenah, Wisconsin

732 Crown Zellerbach
San Francisco

733 McDowell Wellman Engineering Co.
Cleveland

734 Atlas Chemical Industries, Inc.

735 The Setwell Corp.
Traverse City, Michigan

736 Sargent-Welch Scientific Co.
Skokie, Illinois

737

741

738

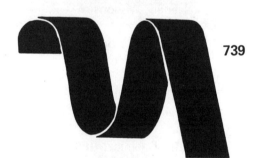

742

739

743

740

744

737 Vargas Zippers
Los Angeles

738 Cargill
Minneapolis

739 Motion Picture Film Services, Inc.
Pittsburgh

740 International Design Center
Minneapolis

741 Neiman Construction Co.
Los Angeles

742 Cal Mode Contract Furniture Mfrs.
Culver City, California

743 Capital National Bank
Houston

744 San Francisco International
Market Center
San Francisco

745 Sport Magazine
Bartell-Media Corp.
New York City

746 Triplett Corporation
Bluffton, Ohio

747 Economic Research Associates, Inc.
Los Angeles

748 Penn Central Transportation Co.
Philadelphia

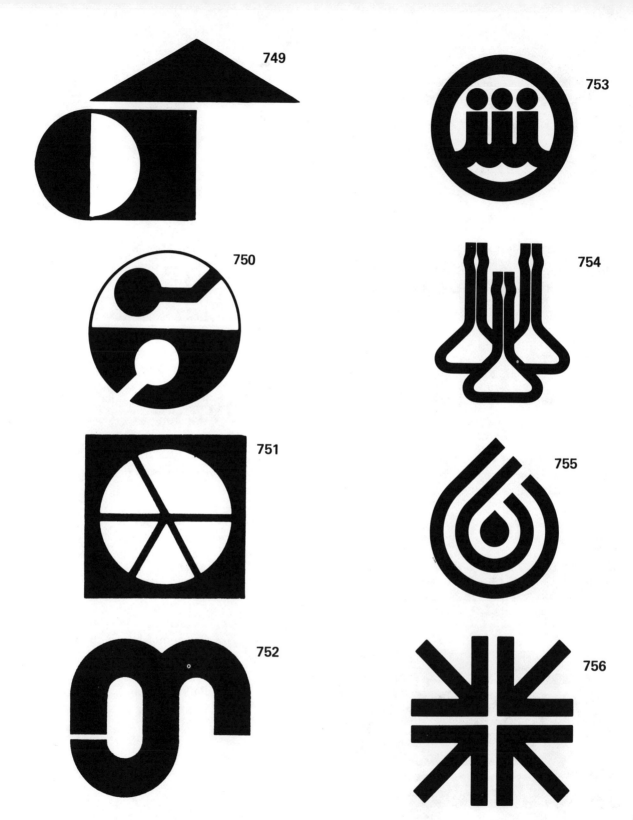

749

753

750

754

751

755

752

756

757

758

759

760

749 Cemcar Co.
Hackensack, New Jersey

750 Lumatrol Co.
Midland Park, New Jersey

751 Mary Friley, Inc.
Financial Consultants
New York City

752 Jack H. Morgan, Architect
Dallas

753 Illumination Industries, Inc.
Sunnyvale, California

754 Bio Science Laboratory
Van Nuys, California

755 Barkow Petroleum
Richmond, California

756 Recognition Devices
Great Neck, New York

757 National Hospital Corp.
Los Angeles

758 Magellan Ltd.
Los Angeles

759 Operation Match
New York City

760 Santa Anita Consolidated, Inc.
Los Angeles

 761

 765

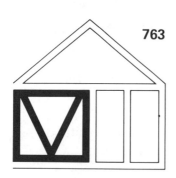 762

 766

 763

 767

 764

 768

769

770

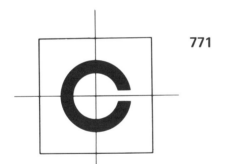

771

772

761 Massachusetts Financial Services, Inc.
Boston

762 U.S. Air Force Systems Command
Washington, D.C.

763 The Vitriform Corp.
Orange, California

764 Financial Congeneric, Inc.
Los Angeles

765 Interactive Data Services
New York City

766 Torin Corporation
Torrington, Connecticut

767 Massachusetts Bay Transportation Authority
Boston

768 Indian Head, Inc.
New York City

769 Peter Kenner Photography
New York City

770 Liquid Paper Corp.
Dallas

771 Calumet Mfg. Co.
Chicago

772 Tioga Pipe Supply Co., Inc.
Philadelphia

773

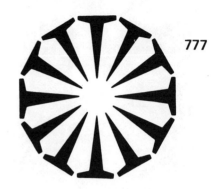

777

774

778

775

779

776

780

781

782

783

784

773 Amcap Fund, Inc.
Los Angeles

774 Land Management, Inc.
Porterville, California

775 Dixon Corporation
Briston, Rhode Island

776 Sunbeam Lighting
Los Angeles

777 Tower Manufacturing Co.
(tacks and nails)
Madison, Indiana

778 National Bank of Washington
Washington, D.C.

779 Columbia Pictures Cassettes
New York City

780 Mount Holyoke College
South Hadley, Massachusetts

781 Getz Corporation
San Francisco

782 Masonite Corporation
Chicago

783 Mid-Continent Helicopter Assoc., Inc.
Omaha, Nebraska

784 Electronic Memories, Inc.
Hawthorne, California

785

789

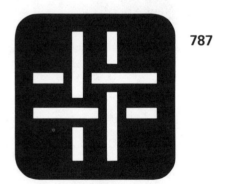

786

790

787

791

788

792

793

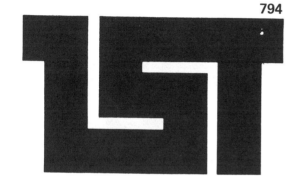

794

795

796

785 The Bellwood Company
Orange, California

786 Converse, Davis & Assoc.
Pasadena, California

787 Burlington Industries
New York City

788 U.S. National Park Service
Harpers Ferry Center
Harpers Ferry, West Virginia

789 National Health Enterprises
Milwaukee

790 Johns Hopkins Press
Baltimore

791 The Signal Companies
Los Angeles

792 Soiltest, Inc.
Evanston, Illinois

793 Saxon Industries, Inc.
New York City

794 First National Bank of Maryland
Baltimore

795 Cone-Heiden
Seattle, Washington

796 The Raymond Corporation
Greene, New York

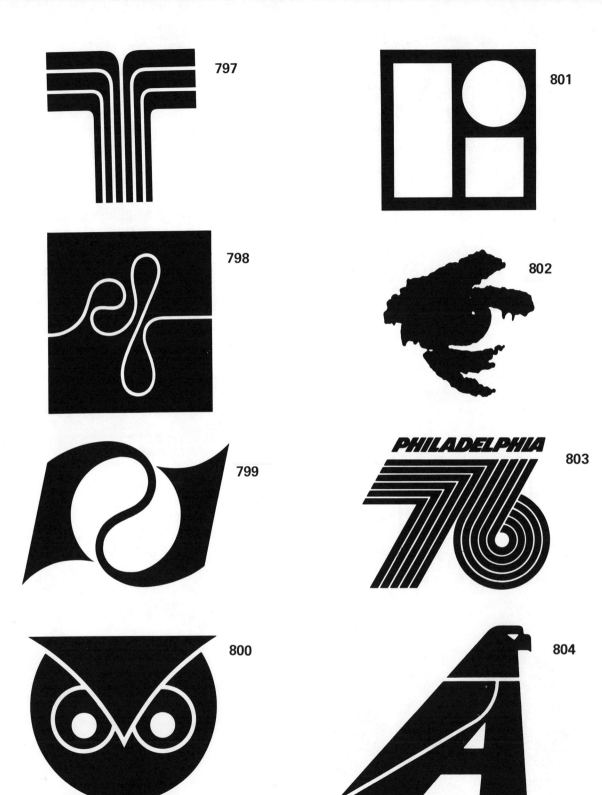

797

801

798

802

799

PHILADELPHIA
76
803

800

804

 **805**

797 Transamerica Corporation
Los Angeles

798 Encounter Films
New York City

799 Major League Baseball
Office of the Commissioner
New York City

800 Fowler & More & Co.
Englewood, Colorado

801 Litton Industries
Beverly Hills, California

802 Curt Cole Burkhart
Chicago

803 Philadelphia Bicentennial Committee
Philadelphia

804 American Stencil Mfg. Co.
Denver

805 Hunt-Wesson Foods, Inc.
Fullerton, California

806 Bank of the Southwest
Houston

807 Omark Industries
Portland, Oregon

808 General Graphics
San Francisco

 **806**

 **807**

 **808**

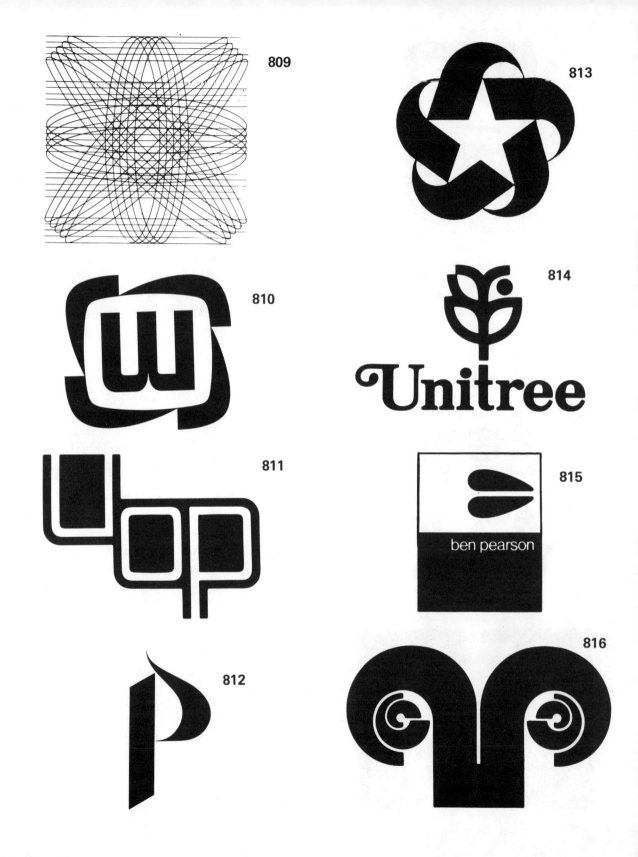

809

813

810

814

Unitree

811

815

ben pearson

812

816

817

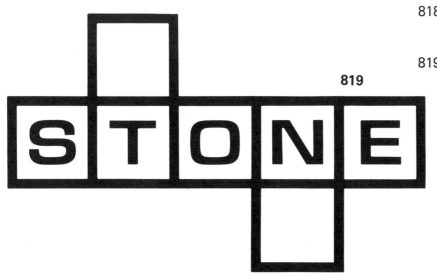

818

819

809 Manhattan School of Music
New York City

810 Waring Products Division
New Hartford, Connecticut

811 Universal Oil Products
Des Plaines, Illinois

812 Pierce Pre-Cooked Foods
Moorefield, West Virginia

813 Clarendon Trust Co.
Arlington, Virginia

814 Unitree
Cheektowaga, New York

815 Ben Pearson Archery
Pine Bluff, Arkansas

816 Sea Ranch
San Francisco

817 Jack's at the Beach
Seafood Restaurant
Santa Monica, California

818 Detroit Bank & Trust
Detroit

819 Stone Container Corp.
Chicago

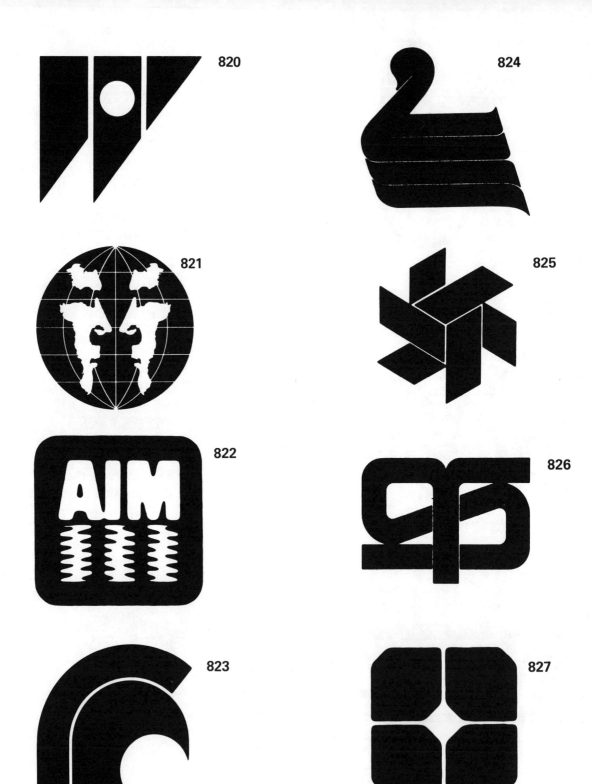

820

824

821

825

822

823

826

827

828

829

830

831

820 Worcester Center
Worcester, Massachusetts

821 Face to Face
The Adams Group
Silver Spring, Maryland

822 American Innerspring Mfrs.
Memphis, Tennessee

823 Trojan Yacht
Lancaster, Pennsylvania

824 Park Bellevue Apartments

825 Northstar at Tahoe
Ski Resort

826 Taxshield
San Francisco

827 Old Stone Bank
Providence, Rhode Island

828 Minter Homes Corporation
Huntington, West Virginia

829 United Missouri Bancshares, Inc.
Kansas City

830 Federal Envelope Division of
Champion Papers
New York City

831 LaMonte-Shimberg Corp.
Tampa, Florida

832

836

833

837

834

838

835

839

 **840**

 **841**

 **842**

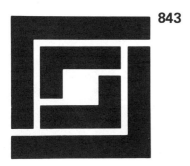 **843**

832 City Investing Co.
New York City

833 InfoServ Corp.
Peoria, Illinois

834 Damon Corporation
Needham, Heights, Massachusetts

835 Meinhard-Commercial Corporation
New York City

836 Color Control Co.
Ft. Lee, New Jersey

837 Urban Systems, Inc.
Cambridge, Massachusetts

838 Institute of Management Sciences
Schaumburg, Illinois

839 Marvin Atkins & Associates
North Hollywood, California

840 Merrimack Valley Textile Museum
North Andover, Massachusetts

841 Western Savings & Loan Association
Phoenix, Arizona

842 Coordinating Council for Higher Education
Sacremento, California

843 Forel
New York City

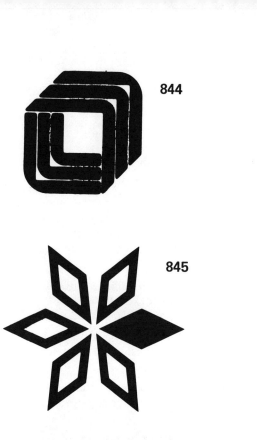

844

848

845

849

846

850

847

851

852

853

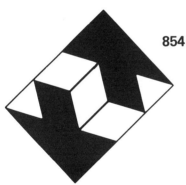

854

855

844 Associated Credit Bureaus
     Houston

845 Diamond Crystal Salt Co.
     St. Clair, Michigan

846 Pacific Lighting Corp.
     Los Angeles

847 Allergan Pharmaceuticals
     Santa Ana, California

848 Rhode Island Arts Festival
     Providence, Rhode Island

849 Dalco Chemical Corp.
     Minneapolis

850 Carl E. Erickson
     Chicago

851 Southland Corporation
     Dairies Division
     Dallas

852 Laguna Niguel Corp.
     Laguna Niguel, California

853 Short Line, Inc.
     Providence, Rhode Island

854 National Association of the
     Partners of the Americas
     Washington, D.C.

855 Safety Management Magazine
     A.M. Best Company
     Morristown, New Jersey

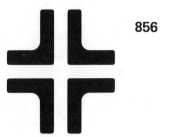

856

860

857

861

858

862

859

863

 864

 865

 866

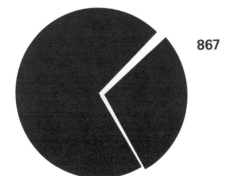 867

856 Louisville Area Chamber of Commerce
Louisville, Kentucky

857 Merrill, Lynch, Pierce, Fenner & Smith
New York City

858 Charles Jourdan Salon
New York City

859 Groos National Bank
San Antonio

860 Purdue Airlines, Inc.
West Lafayette, Indiana

861 Southern California Edison Co.
Los Angeles

862 Homestead Federal Savings & Loan
Dayton, Ohio

863 Princeton Gamma-Tech

864 Sybron Corporation
Rochester, New York

865 Beech Mountain
Banner Elk, North Carolina

866 Worthington Foods
Worthington, Ohio

867 Cordage of Cincinnati
Cincinnati

868

872

869

873

870

874

871

875

876

SIMPSON LEE PAPER COMPANY

877

deepsea

878

879

868 Dallas Baptist College
Dallas

869 Bergstrom Paper Co.
Neenah, Wisconsin

870 Spear & Staff
Babson Park, Massachusetts

871 Marcona Corporation
San Francisco

872 Playhouse Pictures
Hollywood, California

873 Jay Peak (ski village)
Jay, Vermont

874 Hartford National Bank & Trust Co.
Hartford, Connecticut

875 Johnson Reprint Corporation
New York City

876 Simpson Lee Paper Co.
San Francisco

877 First Exchange National Bank
Roanoke, Virginia

878 Deepsea Ventures, Inc.
Gloucester Point, Virginia

879 Piedmont Trust Bank
Martinsville, Virginia

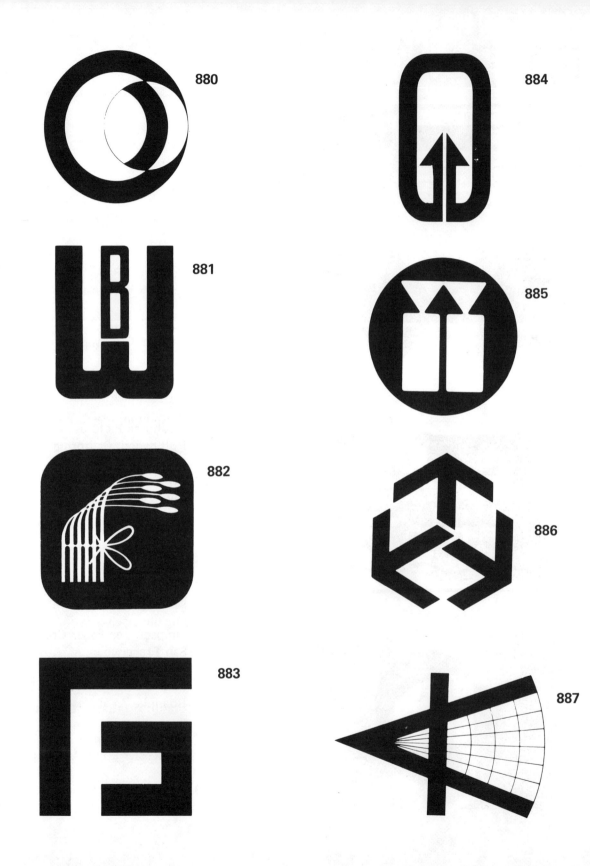

880

884

881

885

882

886

883

887

FAIRMONT 888

889

890

891

880 Optical Products Division of
Aleon Laboratories, Inc.

881 Bryon Weston Co.
Dalton, Massachusetts

882 Foulds Macaroni
Libertyville, Illinois

883 Gregory Fosella Associates
Boston

884 Crown Controls Corp.
New Bremen, Ohio

885 Infotron, Inc.
Burlington, Massachusetts

886 Bank Building Corporation
St. Louis

887 Klein Associates
Salem, New Hampshire

888 Fairmont Foods Co.
Omaha, Nebraska

889 Apex Business Systems, Inc.
Flushing, New York

890 Cryogenic Technology, Inc.
Waltham, Massachusetts

891 Cranford-Johnson & Associates
Little Rock, Arkansas

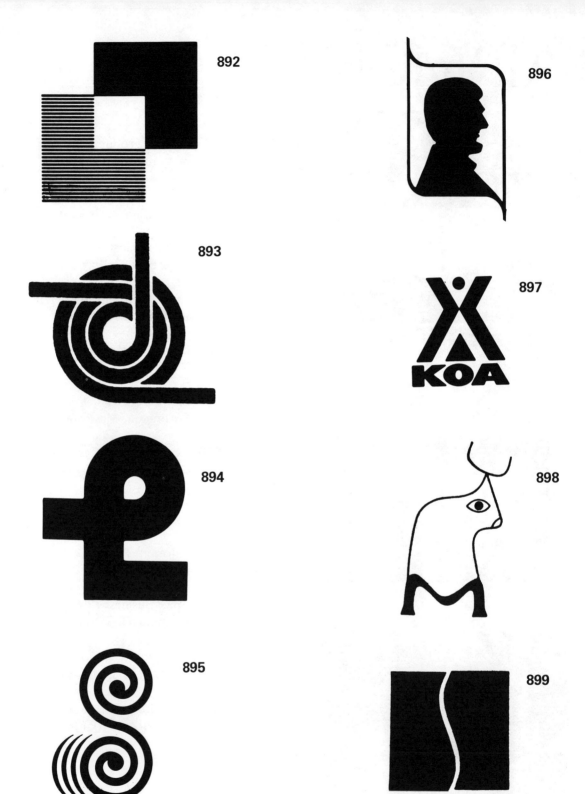

892

896

893

897

KOA

894

898

895

899

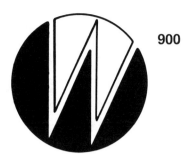 900

 901

 902

903

892 Provident Mutual Life Insurance Co.
Philadelphia

893 Oceanic Properties
Honolulu

894 Learning Corporation of America
New York City

895 E.F. Schmidt Co. Lithographers
Milwaukee

896 Lincoln Trail Bank
Fairview, Illinois

897 Kampgrounds of America
Billings, Montana

898 Museum Books, Inc.
New York City

899 Silver's
Highland Park, Michigan

900 Watson Mfg.
Jamestown, New York

901 Wood Electric Corporation
Danvers, Massachusetts

902 Imperial Bank
Beverly Hills, California

903 Butler Mfg. Co.
Kansas City

904

908

905

909

906

910

907

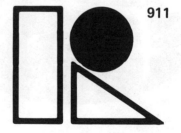

911

912

913

914

915

904 Hollister, Incorporated
Chicago

905 Beldon Roofing & Remodeling
San Antonio, Texas

906 Statler Tissue Corp.
Medford, Massachusetts

907 Ohio University Press
Athens, Ohio

908 Plan Hold
Los Angeles

909 Akro Corporation
Canton, Ohio

910 General Boushelle Inc.
Chicago

911 Richard P. Rita Personnel System
Hartford, Connecticut

912 Oregon Handling Equipment Co.
Portland, Oregon

913 Koch Products

914 Anchor Fence
Baltimore

915 Electronic Voice, Inc.
Los Angeles

 916

 920

 917

 921

 918

 922

 919

 923

 924

 925

 926

 927

916 Evergreen State Builders, Inc.
Tacoma, Washington

917 Fernstrom Moving System
Rosemont, Illinois

918 Bank of Commerce
Tulsa, Oklahoma

919 Intergold Corp.
Albany, New York

920 Youngstown Steel
Youngstown, Ohio

921 Polaris Enterprises, Inc.
Chicago

922 Amprobe Instrument
Lynnbrook, New York

923 Microdot Inc.
Los Angeles

924 U.S. Plywood
New York City

925 Collins Radio Co.
Dallas

926 Balance Technology, Inc.
Ann Arbor, Michigan

927 Armco Steel Corp.
Middletown, Ohio

928

932

EASTERN

929

933

930

cranfil gallery

934

931

935

936

937

Entertainment World

938

EAT•N

939

cGCc GENERAL CINEMA CORPORATION

928 The Louitt Corporation
Providence, Rhode Island

929 Ashland Area Chamber
of Commerce
Ashland, Kentucky

930 MIT Lincoln Laboratory
Lexington, Massachusetts

931 WGN Television
Chicago

932 Eastern Airlines
New York City

933 Westinghouse
Pittsburgh

934 Cranfill Gallery
Dallas

935 Pitney Bowes
Stamford, Connecticut

936 Connecticut General Life Ins. Co.
Hartford

937 Entertainment World Magazine

938 Eaton Corporation
Cleveland

939 General Cinema Corporation

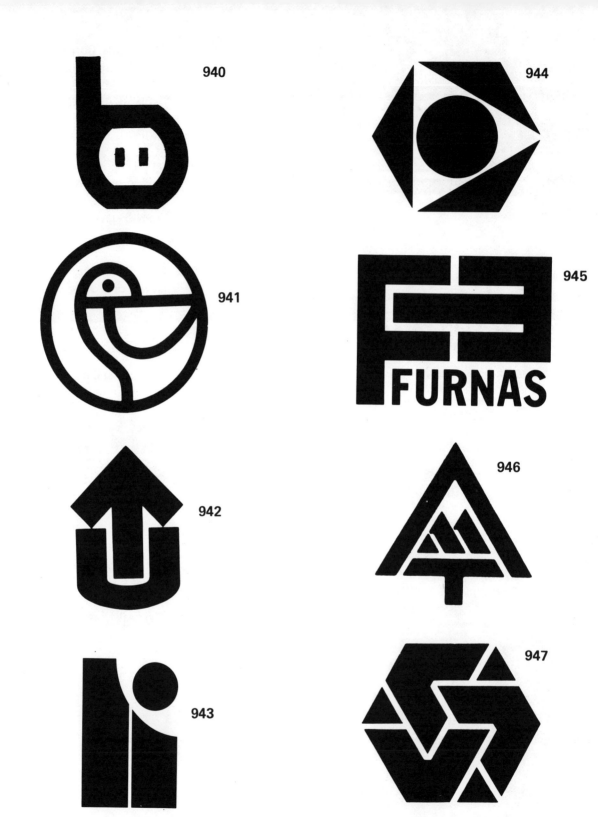

940

944

941

945

FURNAS

942

946

943

947

 948

 949

 950

 951

940 Berg Electric Corporation
Los Angeles

941 Pelican Productions
New York City

942 Uptrend
Trend Industries
Atlanta

943 Harbor Industries, Inc.
Grant Haven, Michigan

944 Hoerner Waldorf Corporation
St. Paul, Minnesota

945 Furnas Electric Corporation
Batavia, Illinois

946 Title Insurance Co. of Minnesota
Minneapolis

947 The Bank of Virginia

948 3M Company
St. Paul, Minnesota

949 Worthen Bank & Trust Co.
Little Rock, Arkansas

950 Ben Koolin Studio
New Burnswick, New Jersey

951 Modine Mfg. Co.
Racine, Wisconsin

952

953

954

955

956

957

952 Equitable Life Insurance Co. of Iowa
Des Moines, Iowa

953 Washington Natural Gas Company
Seattle, Washington

954 Teletype Corporation

955 Allpak Container, Inc.
Seattle, Washington

956 D.H. Overmyer Co., Inc.
New York City

957 Schenck Trebel Corporation
Farmingdale, L.I., New York

958 World Carpets
Dalton, Georgia

958

WORLD CARPETS

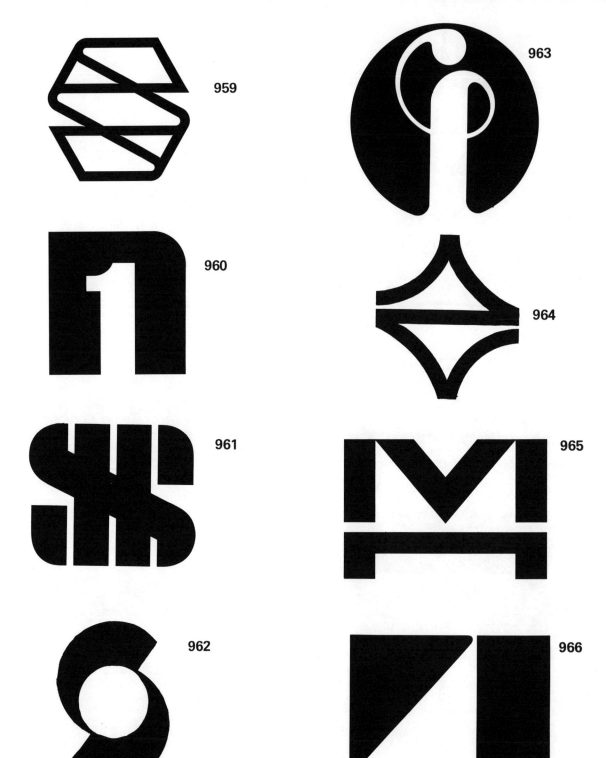

959

960

961

962

963

964

965

966

967

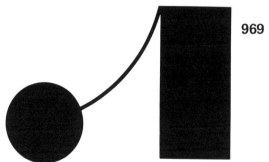

968

969

970

959 Sierracin Corporation
Sun Valley, California

960 National First Corporation
Santa Ana, California

961 Shearson Hammill & Co.

962 Sturm Machine Co., Inc.
Barboursville, West Virginia

963 Inmarco, Inc.
Los Angeles

964 B.C. Ziegler and Co.
West Bend, Wisconsin

965 Mohawk Paper Mills
Cohoes, New York

966 American Motors
Detroit

967 Republic Corporation
Los Angeles

968 United Virginia Bank

969 American Demolition
Denver

970 Diners Club
New York City

 971

 975

 972

 976

 973

 977

 974

 978

979

980

981

982

971 Brentwood Sportswear
New York City

972 American Can Co.
New York City

973 North Carolina Mutual Life Insurance Co.
Durham, North Carolina

974 Deposit Guaranty National Bank
Jackson, Mississippi

975 Rand McNally & Co.
Chicago

976 The Hamm Brewing Co.
St. Paul, Minnesota

977 PPG Industries
Pittsburgh

978 Hercules Incorporated
Wilmington, Delaware

979 FMR Corporation
West Haven, Connecticut

980 Xerox Corporation
Rochester, New York

981 Sanders Associates
Nashua, New Hampshire

982 Mobil Oil Corp.
New York City

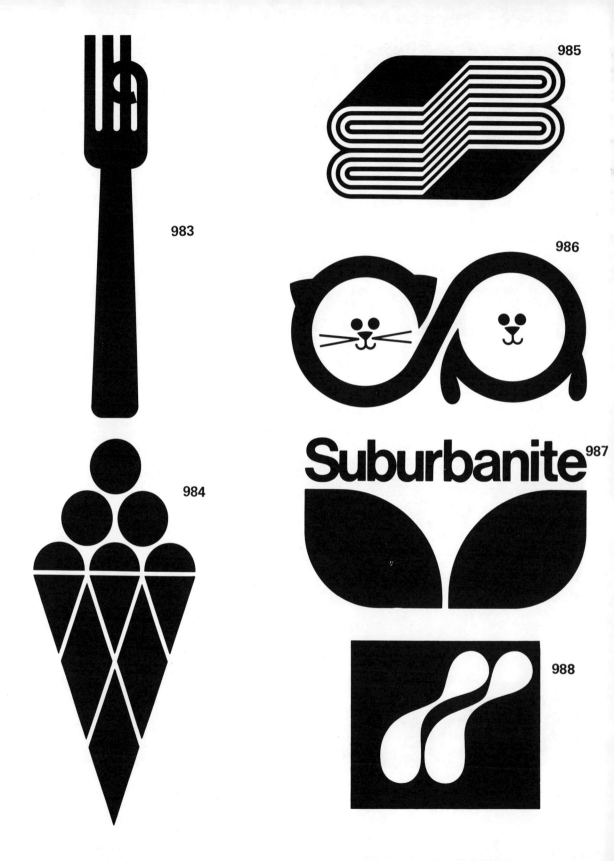

983

984

985

986

Suburbanite 987

988

989

990

991

992

983 9 Muses Restaurant
Los Angeles

984 James McManus Corp.
(ice cream manufacturer)
Quincy, Massachusetts

985 Brown University Press
Providence, Rhode Island

986 Animal Rescue League
Boston

987 Suburbanite Mop Co.
Brookline, Massachusetts

988 Price Pfister Brass Mfg. Co.
Los Angeles

989 Kenroy Inc.
Skokie, Illinois

990 American Actuaries, Inc.
Chicago

991 Kings Lafayette Bank
Brooklyn

992 Pacific Theatres
Los Angeles

Index

Abbott Laboratories, 561
Abex Corporation, 584
Academy of Art College, 513
Acheson Colloids Company, 8
Achshnet Company, 654
Additive "A", Kimberly Clark, 731
Advance Mortgage Corporation, 138
Aero Bankers, 366
Aerojet Liquid Rocket Co., 480
Aerospace Corporation, 588
Aerostar — Ted Smith Aircraft
    Company, Inc., 107
Aerotron, Inc. 556
Agricultural Missions, Inc. 314
Air Products & Chemicals, Inc., 98
Aircraft Radio Corporation, 438
Ajax Hardware Corporation, 359
Ajax Magnathermatic Corp., 126
Akro Corporation, 909
Albright-Knox Art Gallery, 398
Alcan Corporation, 246
Allergan Pharmaceuticals, 847
Allied Casting Corporation, 226
Allpak Container, Inc., 955
Alpine State Bank, 632
Aluminum Association, The, 313
Aluminum Corporation of
    America, 716
Amcap Fund, Inc. 773
American Actuaries, Inc., 990
American Bankers Association, 381
American Building Maintenance
    Industries, 711
American Can Company, 972
American Cast Iron Pipe Co., 341
American Demolition, 969
American Exporter, 248
American Film Institute, 690
American Forest Institute, 445
American Greetings Corporation,
    177
American Innerspring Manufacturers,
    822
American Institute of Architects, 397
American Journal of Nursing, 159
American Motors, 966

American National Bank & Trust, 572
American Protection Industries, 67
American Republic Insurance Co., 263
American Revolution Bicentennial
    Commission, 14
American Sentry Corporation, 127
American Stencil Manufacturing Co.,
    804
American Tube & Controls Inc., 78
Amplex Manufacturing Co., 416
Amprobe Instrument, 922
Anchor Fence, 914
Anderson Corporation, 703
Animal Rescue League, 986
Anixter Bros., Inc., 724
Ansul Co., The, 553
Antilles Yachting Service, 675
Anzio, 354
Apex Business Systems, Inc., 889
Applied Logic Corporation, 295
Applied Power Industries, Inc., 374
Aquaria, Inc., 62
Aragon International, Inc., 275
Arapahoe Earth Movers, 245
Architectural Design Assoc., 198
Architectural Pottery, 273
Arkansas Industrial Development
    Commission, 276
Arkwright-Interlaken, Inc., 607
Arlen Realty & Development Corp.,
    670
Armco Steel Corporation, 927
Armour-Dial, Inc. , 510
Art's Photo, 729
Asgrow Seed Company, 306
Ashland Area Chamber of
    Commerce, 929
Aspen Skiing Corporation, 131
Associated Credit Bureaus, Inc., 844
Associated Spring Co., 321
Marvin Atkins & Associates, 839
Atlantic National Bank, 720
Atlantic Richfield Co., 110
Atlas Chemical Industries, Inc., 734
Atlas Van Lines, 570.
Balance Technology, 926

Bangor Punta Corporation, 501
Bank of America, 713
Bank Building Corporation, 886
Bank of the Commonwealth, 162
Bank of the Commonwealth, 614
Bank of Commerce, 387
Bank of Commerce, 918
Bank of Maine, 611
Bank Marketing Association, 565
Bank Printing Co., Inc., 585
Bank of the Southwest, 806
Bank of Virginia, The, 947
Bankers Life, The, 683
Bankers Trust, 133
Barden Corp., The, 335
Barkow Petroleum, 755
Barr Chemical Products, Inc., 539
Baseler Photo Marketing Co., Inc.,
    187
Bauer & Black, 609
Bay State Abrasives, 345
Beam-Cast, Inc., 261
Beaunit Corp., 242
Beaver Cove, 193
Beaver Cove Marina, 194
Beech Mountain, 865
Beekman Downtown Hospital, 25
Behlen Manufacturing Co., 353
Beldon Roofing & Remodeling, 905
Bell Brand Foods, 238
Bell Records, 449
Bellarmine College, 554
Bellwood Co., The, 785
Berg Electric Corp., 940
Berg Hayslette, 681
Bergstrom Paper Co., 869
Berley Industries, Inc., 463
Berven Carpets Corp., 648
Beverly Hills Bankcorp, 125
Beverly Hills Tennis Club, 24
Bianco Manufacturing Co., 91
Bio Science Laboratory, 754
Bird Precision Jewels, 602
Birdsall, John, Creative Services, 50
Blakeslee-Lane Photography, 23
Boise Cascade Corporation, 772

Boise Cascade Corp., 772
Boles Aero, Inc., 317
Books Unlimited, 33
Boothe Resources, Intl., Inc. 401
Brammer's Business Interiors, 175
Brazos Graphics, 725
Brennan & Slone Construction Co., 368
Brentwood Sportswear, 971
Brite Industries, 277
Bronwill Scinetific, Inc., 340
Broward Bankshares, Inc., 315
Brown-Foreman Distillers, 297
Brown University Press, 985
Bryant Press, 215
Bryon Weston Co., 881
Buffalo Savings Bank, 102
The Bunker-Ramo Corporation, 666
Burkhart, Curt Cole, 802
Burks Pumps, 517
Burlington Industries, 787
Burlington Northern, 217
Burns & Towne, 192
Burns, William J. Detective Agency,
   347
Butler Manufacturing Co., 903
CBS, 18
Cal Mode Contract Furniture
   Manufacturers, 742
California Casulaty Insurance Group,
   529
California Products Corp., 141
Calumet Manufacturing Co., 771
Cameron Machine Co., 407
Camp Rafa-El, Marin Jewish
   Community Center, 3
Canadian Waters, Inc., 54
Canfield, M.C. Sons, 73
Capital Group, The, Inc., 464
Capital National Bank, 743
Capital National Corp., 741
Capitol Records, 38
Carborundum Co., The, 108
Carefree Services, 82
Cargill, 738
Carlton Screw Mfg. Co., 330
Carrier Envelope Co., 76
Carteret Savings & Loan Assn., 488
Cascade Airways, 140
Cascade Electric, 137
Case, J.I. Co., 700
Celanese Corporation, 564
Cemcar Co., 749
Central Penn National Bank, 132

Central Soya, 370
Charles Industries, 413
Chase Manhattan Bank, The, 508
Cheyenne Mountain Ranch, 642
Children's Press, 628
Chrysler Corporation, 702
Citizens Federal Savings & Loan
   Association, 486
Citizens Fidelity Bank, 233
Citizens National Bank, 22
City Investing Co., 832
City National Bank, 43
Clarendon Trust Co., 813
Clark, J.L., 338
Clarksville Theatre, 255
Clay & Adams, 204
Cleveland Institute of Art, 319
Cleveland Trust, 309
Clevepak Corporation, 394
Coherent Radiation Laboratories,
   477
College/University Corporation, 100
Collins Radio Co., 925
Colonie Center, 698
Color Control Co., 836
Color Concentrate Corp., 606
Color Service, Inc., 106
Colorado National Bank, 269
Colt Industries, 519
Columbia Pictures, 779
Comerco, Inc., 441
Comlab, Inc., 512
Committee of Arts & Lectures,
   University of California, 536
Community Banks of Washington,
   The, 444
Community Relations Center, 265
Computer Knowledge Corp., 393
Computer Products, 375
Cone-Heiden, 795
Connecticut General Life Insurance
   Company, 936
Consolidated International Corp., 656
Consumer Alliance, 541
Continental Airlines, 706
The Continental Bank, 188
Continental Steel Corporation, 674
Contract Interiors, Inc., 555
Converse, Davis & Associates, 786
Conwed Corporation, 172
Cooper Tool Co., 26
Coordinating Council for Higher
   Education, 842

Cordage of Cincinnati, 867
Cordon International Corp., 239
Cornnuts, Inc., 548
Corporate Communications Co., Inc.,
   251
Gray & Rogers, Corporate Identities
   Division, 203
Corpus Christi Bank & Trust, 183
Cousins Properties, Inc., 491
Arthur Cox & Sons., Inc., 447
Cranfill Gallery, 934
Cranford-Johnson & Associates, 891
Creative Equity Corp., 213
Creative Packaging, 679
Crossett Company, The., 115
Crown Controls Corp., 884
Crown Paper, 618
Crown Zellerbach, 732
Cryogenic Technology, Inc., 890
Crystal Shores, 534
Culligan, Inc., 369
Dalco Chemical Corp., 849
Dallas Baptist College, 868
Damon Corporation, 834
Data Network Corporation, 461
Dayton Hudson Corporation, 597
Dayton Typographic Service, 563
Deepsea Ventures, Inc., 878
Decatur Income Fund, 46
Decker Clarke Corporation, The, 58
Deere & Co., 392
Delaware Fund, 48
Delaware Management Co., Inc., 45
Delaware River Port Authority, 686
Delray Dunes Golf & Country Club,
   182
Delta Trend Fund, 47
Deposit Guaranty National Bank,
   874
Detroit Bank & Trust, 818
Diamond Crystal Salt Co., 845
Diamond Shamrock Corp., 378
Dickenson Publishing Co., Inc.,
   156
Diehl Pump Co., 414
DiGiorgio Development Corp.,
   712
Diners Club, 970
Direct Mail Advertising Association,
   569
Directional Industries, Inc., 396
Directions or Dilemmas, 689
Ditto, Inc., 620

Diversey Corporation, 601
Diversified Products Co., 657
Dixon Corporation, 775
Dodge Cork Co., 466
Dot Records, 708
Draper, Charles Stark, Laboratory of MIT, 439
Ducommun Incorporated, 117
Ducommun Metals & Supply Company, 118
Dukane Press, 390
Duquesne Light, 549
Durst Organization, The, 112
Dynastructures, Inc., 228
ECL Industries, 499
EG&G, 353
East Dayton Tool & Die Co., 283
Eastern Airlines, 932
Eastern Stainless Steel Co., 643
Eaton Corp., 938
Economic Development Corp. of San Diego County, 339
Economics Research Associates, Inc., 747
Edgewood Furniture Co., Inc., 209
Edinger-Wyckoff, Inc., 578
Edmund Scientific Co., 380
Educreative Systems, Inc., 485
Eidophor Inc., Division of CIBA, 212
Eisert Racing Enterprises, Inc., 164
EKCO Products, Inc., 111
Electronic Memories, Inc., 784
Electronic Voice, Inc., 915
Electrovision Productions, Inc., 547
Emhart Corporation, 56
Encounter Films, 798
Entertainment World Magazine, 937
Envirotech Corporation, 41
Enviromental Measurements, Inc., 478
Equitable Life Insurance Co., of Iowa, 952
Equitable Trust Bank, 559
Equity Funding Corp. of America, 97
Erfft Associates, Inc., 227
Erickson, Carl E., 850
Everbrite Electric Signs, Inc., 673

Evergreen State Builders, Inc., 916
Evers Savings Association, 604
Ex-Cell-O Corporation, 524
Excellon Industries, 671
Exolon Co., The, 240
FMR Corp., 979
Face-to-Face, 821
Facit-Ohner, Inc., 236
Fains Floor Covering, 218
Fairmont Foods Co., 888
Family Funding, Inc., 676
Farmlands USA, 459
Federal Compress & Warehouse Co., 146
Federal Envelope, Division of Champion Papers, 830
Federal Mogul, 682
Fernstrom Moving System, 917
Financial Congeneric, Inc., 764
Finn Industries, 145
First Exchange National Bank, 877
First National Bank, 144
First National Bank, 184
First National Bank, 437
First National Bank, 515
First National Bank, 558
First National Bank in Little Rock, 382
First National Bank of Maryland, 794
First National Bank of Minneapolis, 234
First National Bank in Palm Beach, 79
First Union National Bank, 70
Flex-Weld, Inc., 281
Florissant Land Development, 249
Follett Corporation, 173
Follett Educational Corp., 20
Foothill General Corporation, 80
Ford Wire Products, 633
Forel, 843
Foremost Lithograph, 605
Form & Function, 428
Fosella, Gregory Assoc., 883
Foster Parents Plan, Inc., 372
Fosters Meats, 406
Fould's Macaroni, 882
Four-Phase Systems, Inc., 293
Fourth National Bank, 57
Fowler & More & Co., 800
Franklin Interiors, 63
Franklin Supply Co., 432

Franklin Town, 37
Franklin Typographers, 500
J. F. Freeman, Inc., 424
W.H. Freeman & Co., Publishers, 180
Fremerman-Papin, Inc., 448
Frilay, Mary, Inc., 751
Fuller-O'Brien Corp., 287
Fun Stop, 304
Furnas Electric Corp., 945
G.A.C. Corp., 599
GATX, 2
Gallmeyer & Livingston Co., 52
Gate City Steel, 634
Gates Aviation Corp., 709
Gelman Instrument Co., 235
Gelpe, Sid & Assoc., Landscape Designers, 658
General Boushelle, Inc., 910
General Cinema Corp., 939
General Fireproofing Co., The, 13
General Graphics, 808
General Learning Corp, 77
General Oceanography, 476
Genesco, 701
Gettysburg Urban Renewal, 229
Getz Corp., 781
Gillette Toiletries, 189
Girard Bank, 423
Glass Containers Corp., 645
Globus, L.J. Advertising, Inc., 574
Goodall Rubber Co., 624
Goodwill Industries, 200
Gordo Records, 109
Goren Foods Co., 346
Gottesman Central National Corp., 691
Gould, Inc., 593
Gould's Pumps, 101
Government in the Modern World, Macmillan Co., 433
Gradison, W.D. & Co., 44
Graphic Communications, 331
Graphics Studio, The, 291
Gravely Corp., 312
Grayrock Oil & Gas, 431
Great Northwest Federal Savings & Loan Association, 446
Greater Washington Jewish Community Foundation, 422
Groos National Bank, 859

Grossman Publishers, 521
Growth Fund of American, Inc., 457
HMH Publishing Co., 467
Hagemeister-Lert, Inc., 532
Halliday & Blalock, Inc., 409
Hamm Brewing Co., The, 976
Shearson Hammill & Co., 961
Hancock-Gross, 148
Hankscraft, 342
Harbor Industries, Inc., 943
Hartford Hospital, 103
Hartford National Bank & Trust Co., 874
Hartford Public Library, 171
Harwood House, 150
Hawaii Production Center, 490
Hawaiian Wines, Inc., 266
Haystack Ski Area, 195
Head Ski Co., Inc., 289
Heatilator Fireplaces, Vega Industries, 116
Helbros Watches, 323
Helipot Division, Bechman Instruments, 621
Hennessey Three Star Industries, 452
Hercules, Inc., 978
Higgins Hegner Genovese, Inc., 580
Hitchiner Mfg. Co., Inc., 672
Hoerner Waldorf Corp., 944
Hoffman-Taff, Inc., 473
Holiday Airlines, 89
Hollister, Inc., 904
Hollywood Car Wash, 677
Homestead Federal Savings & Loan Association, 862
Hooker Chemical Corp., 124
Hoppe's, 86
Hospicare, Inc., 589
Houghton Chemical Corp., 197
House of Fabrics, Inc., 253
House of Ronnie, Inc., 352
Howell Design Associates, 29
Hunt-Wesson Foods, Inc., 805
Huntly Gaming Co., 190
IBM, 205
Illinois Central Railroad, 678
Illumination Industries, Inc., 753
Imaginetics, Inc., 104
Imperial Bank, 902
Imperial International Learning, 19
Income Fund of America, Inc., 458
Indian Head, Inc., 768
Industrial Design Collaborative, 163

Industrial Agricolas, 241
Information International, 128
Info Serv Corporation, 833
Infoton, Inc., 885
Ingram Paper Co., 388
Ink, Inc., 42
Inmarco, Inc., 963
Innerspace Environments, Inc., 66
Innovation House, Inc., 456
Institute of Management Sciences, 838
Insurance Co., of North America, 410
Inter-Faith Task Force, 288
Interactive Data Services, 765
Intergold Corp., 919
International Applied Science Laboratory, 65
International Design Center, 740
International Geomarine Corp., 587
International Instant Archery Assn., 279
International Minerals & Chemicals, 59
International Paper Co., 475
Intertechnique, 40
Isramet Trading Corp., 28
Jack's at the Beach, 817
Jacks 4, 130
Jalart House, 695
Janet Rosenblum, Inc., 30
Jay Peak, 873
Jefferson National Bank, 181
Jeffries Banknote Co., 613
Jeppesen & Co., 123
Johns Hopkins Press, 790
Johnson Foils, Inc., 139
Mead Johnson Laboratories, 581
Johnson Reprint Corp., 875
Charles Jourdan Salon, 858
KSTP Television, 636
Kallir, Philips, Ross, Inc., 722
Kampgrounds of America, 897
Kasparians, Inc., 36
Keepper Nagel, Inc., 68
Keller Williams Furniture Mfg. Co., 577
Kendall Co., The, 355
Kenner, Peter, Photography, 769
Kenroy, Inc., 989
Kentucky Electric Steel Co., 504
Keuffel & Esser Co., 627
Kierulff Electronics, 119
Kimberly-Clark Corp., 511
Kings Lafayette Bank, 991

Kirsch Co., The, 582
Klein Associates, 887
Klopman Mills, 191
Knapp Bros. Shoe Manufacturers, 692
Koch Products, 913
Koolin, Ben, Studio, 950
Koracorp Industries, 560
Kovler Gallery, 579
LaBow, Haynes Co., Inc., 400
La Choy Food Products, 367
Laco Signs, Inc., 332
Laguna Niguel Corp., 852
Lake Forest National Bank, 16
LaMonte-Shimberg Corp., 831
Land Management, Inc., 774
Land Search Corp., 344
Larson Enterprises, Inc., 257
Larwin Group, The, Inc., 94
LaSalle Steel, 610
Lassen Volcanic National Park, 482
Lauter-Franklin Road Paving, 420
Lawry's Food, Inc., 185
Lawter Chemicals, Inc., 134
Learning Corp. of America, 894
Leblanc Corp., G., 157
Letterforms, 307
Lincoln Trail Bank, 896
Liquid Paper Corp., 770
Litton Industries, 801
Living Marine Resources, Inc., 356
Loft's Candy Co., 160
Logan Clay Products, 616
Logistics Systems, Inc., 290
Lone Star Industries, Inc., 166
Lord & Burnham, 296
Love, Joseph, & Co., 710
Louisville Area Chamber of Commerce, 856
Louitt Corp., The, 928
Lucas, Jim, Photography, 70
Lumatrol Co., 750
Lummus Co., The, 652
Lutheran Fraternal Organization, 300
McDowell Wellman Engineering Co., 733
McKesson & Robbins Drug Co., 704
McManus, James, Corp., 984
MH&W, 694
MIT Lincoln Laboratory, 930
MIT Press, 371

MPB Corp., 49
Madison Square Garden, 403
Magellan Ltd., 758
Magnus Organ Corp., 730
Maico Hearing Instruments, 425
Main Place, 264
Maine Savings Bank, 365
Major League Baseball, 799
Majors & Majors Realtors, 550
Makaha Inn, 316
Malacanadra Productions, 262
Manhattan School of Music, 809
Marcal Paper Mills, Inc., 21
Marcona Corp., 871
Marine Midland Bank, 219
Marine Sciences, 622
Marine World, 479
Marker-Berry Graphics, 51
Marshall Industries, 252
Martin, Nancy, Public Relations, 364
Martin Senour Paints, 202
Massachusetts Bank & Trust, 143
Massachusetts Bay Transportation
    Authority, 767
Massachusetts Financial Services,
    Inc., 761
Masonite Corporation, 782
Masterlock Co., 715
Matheson Gas Products, 179
Matheson Scientific, 668
Mayell, Norman L. & Associates, 96
Mayfran, Inc., 230
Maytag Co., The, 272
Medalist Industries, 329
Medi Mart, 303
Memphis Area Chamber of
    Commerce, 247
Meinhard-Commercial Corp., 835
Merchandise Display, Inc., 318
Merchants Bank of Allentown, 90
Merchants Indurance Group, 136
Merrill Mfg. Corp., 649
Merrill, Lynch, Pierce, Fenner &
    Smith, 857
Merrimack Valley Textile Museum,
    840
Metals Research Instrument Corp.,
    596
Metropolitan Life Insurance, 468
Metropolitan Wire Goods Corp., 129
Microdot, 923
Mid-Continent Helicopter Associates,
    783

Middle South Services, Inc., 211
Midland Mortgage Co., 651
Midland-Ross Corp., 653
Miller & Fink Publishers, Patient
    Care Projects Div., 455
Miller, Herman, Inc., 270
Miller, T.C., Realty Co., 640
Mills, Cone, Marketing Co., 721
Milwaukee Faucets, Inc., 502
Minter Homes Corp., 828
Mister Donut, 361
Mobil Oil Corp., 982
Modine Mfg. Co., 951
Modular Building, 697
Moen, 405
Mohawk Paper Mills, 965
Monogram Industries, Inc., 551
Montague-Spragens Printers, 537
Montessori Family Center, 220
Moore Business Forms, 336
Morgan, Jack H., Architect, 752
Morris Museum of Arts & Sciences,
    69
Motion Picture Film Services, Inc.,
    739
Motorola, Inc., 231
Mount Attitash Assn., 418
Mount Holyoke College, 780
Mount McKinley National Park, 483
Mountain Sports, 358
Mountz, D.G. Assoc., Inc., 667
Multiples, Inc., 664
Museum Books, Inc., 898
Mutron, 660
Myles, Lee, Assoc., Inc., Adver-
    tising, 74
Myles, Lee, Assoc., Inc., Print-
    ing, 75
Nalco Chemical Co., 552
Nashua Corp., 595
National Association of the Partners
    of the Americas, 854
National Bank, The, 386
National Bank of Commerce, 629
National Bank of Washington, 778
NBC, 376
National Central Bank, 631
National Corporation for Housing
    Partnerships, 591
National Council for Negro Women,
    214
National Elevator, 176
National Energy Systems Corp., 594
National First Corp., 960

National Forest Products Assn., 494
National Health Enterprises, 789
National Hospital Corp., 757
National Railroad Passenger Corp.,
    523
Neiman Construction Co., 741
New England Aquarium, 9
New England Farms, 348
New York Aquarium, 149
New York Life Insurance Co, 232
New York School of Interior Design,
    322
New York State University, 15
New York University Glee Club, 419
Newport Center, 430
Nilsen Group, The, 639
Nine Muses Restaurant, 983
Nor-Lake, Inc., 93
Norgren, C.A. Co., 351
Norstar Sales Inc., 637
North American Rockwell, 310
North American Van Lines, 626
North Carolina Mutual Life Insurance
    Co., 973
Northeast Subway Extension, 592
Northstar at Tahoe Ski Resort, 825
Northwestern National Life Insurance
    Co., 426
Northwest Bankcorporation, 168
Nuclear Data, Inc., 619
Nuclear Pacific, Inc., 493
Nystrom, A.J. & Co., 662
Nytron, Inc., 538
Oakley Tube Corp., 169
Ohio Brass Co., The, 661
Ohio National Bank, 95
Ohio Safety Systems, Inc., 282
Ohio Trailways, 590
Ohio University Press, 907
Ohmite Mfg. Co., 244
Old Stone Bank, 827
Olivetti Underwood Corp., 506
Omark Industries, 807
Omnibus Film Productions, 516
Omniplan, 174
Operation Match, 759
Optical Products Division, Aleon
    Laboratories, Inc., 880
Oceanic Properties, 893
Overmeyer, D.H. Co., Inc., 956
Oxford Papers, 663
PPG Industries, 977
Pace Fund, Stanford University, 540

Pacific Electrical, 71
Pacific Fashion Institute, 646
Pacific Lighting Corp., 846
Pacific National Bank of Washington, 442
Pacific Palm Pools, 404
Pacific Theatres, 992
Panelgraphic Corp., 274
Park Bellevue Apartments, 824
Parker Machine, Inc., 285
Parker Pen Co., 568
Patchcord Productions, Inc., 542
Pathfinder Fund, The, 617
Peace Corps, 53
Pearson, Ben, Archery, 815
Pelican Productions, 941
Pellon Corp., 412
Pembroke's, 61
Penguim Industries, Inc., 85
Penn Central Transportation Co., 748
Pennsylvania, New Jersey, & Delaware Committee of Governors, 299
Penn's Southwest Assn., 487
Pennwalt Corp., 207
People's Bank, 451
People's Bank of Western Pennsylvania, 170
Pepsi Cola International, 495
Perfect Film & Chemical, 498
Perfection Gear Company, 1
Pet, Inc., 707
Phili-tec Division, Western World Electronic Corp., 31
Philadelphia Bicentennial Committee, 803
Philadelphia Chapter, AIA, 225
Philadelphia Diagnostic & Rehabilitation Service, 298
Photographic Display Laboratories, 186
Piedmont Minerals Co., Inc., 395
Piedmont Trust Bank, 879
Pierce Pre-Cooked Foods, 812
Pioneer Electronics USA Corp., 147
Pitney Bowes, 935
Pittsburgh Airways, Inc., 567
Pittsburgh National Bank, 705
Plan Hold, 908
Planning Research, 334
Platt Bros & Co., The, 60
Playhouse Pictures, 872
Precision Plating Co., 520
Presbyterian Hospital Center, 356

Pressman Corp., 496
Price Pfister Brass Mfg. Co., 988
Princeton Gamma-Tech, 863
Problematics, 113
Propinquity, 575
Provident Mutual Life Insurance Co., 892
Prudent Publishing Co., 178
Polaris Enterprises, 921
Pollota & Sommers General Contractors, 114
Polyplan Plastic Products Mfg., 435
Porcelain Studio, 154
Poultry Guild, 333
Public Service Indiana, 55
Purdue Airlines, Inc., 860
Pyttronic, Inc., 373
Quality Cheese & Spice, 142
Quillayote Camp, 492
RCA, 84
Rancho San Diego, 250
Rand McNally & Co., 975
Random House, 271
Raymond Corp., The, 796
Realty Systems, Inc., 684
Recognition Devices, 756
Recognition Equipment, Inc., 7
Recreation Industries, Inc., 460
Red Radish, The, 535
Redactron Corporation, 6
Redwood Bank, 87
Reeves Telecom Corp., 472
Renauld International Ltd., 693
Republic Corporation, 967
Republic Steel Corp., 583
Reynolds, R.J. Industries, 518
Rhode Island Arts Festival, 848
Richmond Research Corp., 152
Rita, Richard P. Personnel Systems, 911
Rochester Institute of Technology, 165
Rohm & Haas Co., 576
Rose Engineering Co., 573
Ross Yacht, 284
Roth Office Environments, 237
Royal Continental Box Co., 377
Royal Industries, 566
SMC Industries, Inc., 325
Safety Management Magazine, A.M. Best Co., 855
Salada Foods, 222

Salem Plaza, 481
Salesvertising Art, 4
San Francisco Experience, The; Electrovision Productions, Inc., 546
San Francisco International Market Center, 744
Sanders Associates, 981
Santa Anita Consolidated, Inc., 760
Sargent-Welch Scientific Co., 736
Sawyer Industries, Inc., 408
Saxon Industries, Inc., 793
Schenck Trebel Corp., 957
Schmidt, E.F. Co., Lithographers, 895
Charles Schnier Development Co., 311
School of Visual Arts, 717
Schorr Brothers, 450
Scientific Resources, 153
Scintillonics, 719
Scintex, Inc., 699
Scott Engineering Sciences, 216
Scott Paper Co., 562
Screen Gems, 644
Screen Gems—Columbia Music, 421
Screen Gems—Columbia Productions, 417
Scubapro Diving Equipment, 434
Sculpture Collectors, Ltd., 337
Sea Ranch, 816
Seatrain Lines, 12
Security Corp., 489
Security First National Bank, 64
Seiberling Tire & Rubber Co., 155
Self Development, Inc., 415
Setwell Corp., 735
Seven Lakes, 638
Sherer-Gillett Co., 294
Short Line, Inc., 853
Shultzy's, 685
Sierracin Corp., 959
Signal Companies, The, 791
Signetics Corporation, 557
Silver's, 899
Simpson Lee Paper Co., 876
Small Circle of Friends, The, 267
Snowbird, Ltd., 167
Soiltest, Inc., 792
Sonoco Products Co., 514
South Carolina National Bank, 301
Southern California Edison, 861

Southern Cross Industries, Inc., 436
Southern Natural Gas Co., 99
Southland Corporation, 680
Southland Corporation, Dairies
    Division, 851
Southwest Forest Industries, 718
Spear & Staff, 870
Spectra Physics, 525
Speedrack, Inc., 389
Sperry Rand Corp., 206
Sperti Sunlamp Division, 221
Spicer Divisions, Dana Corp., 157
Sport Magazine, Bartell-Media Corp.,
    745
Spring '71 Bookfair, 726
Springer-Verlag New York, Inc.,
    158
Squaw Valley Land & Livestock Co.,
    531
Standard & Poors/Inter Capital, Inc.,
    669
Starnes, B.R. Co., 280
Statler Tissue Corp., 906
Steel Service Center Institute, 615
Sterling Answer Service, 308
Stone Container Corporation, 819
Stop & Shop, 302
Stow-Davis Furniture Co., 402
Strathmore Paper Co., 360
Sturm Machine Co., Inc., 962
Suburban Printers, 696
Suburbanite Mop Co., 987
Sun Newspapers, 121
Sun & Powder, Inc., 443
Sunbeam Lighting, 776
Sundial Electronic Corp., 224
Sunnyside Products, Inc., 350
Super-Temp Co., 120
Superior Coach Corp., 399
Surety Savings & Loan Assn., 474
Sutro & Co., Inc., 527
Swedcast Div., Swedlow, Inc., 326
Sybron Corp., 864
Synthane-Taylor Corp., 383
Tab, Coca-Cola Co., 509
Tahoe Keys, 533
Tax Man, 349
Tax Shield, 826
Technical Exhibits Corp., 81
Teledyne, Inc., 83
Teletype Corp., 954
Temple Industries, 470
Tern Contracting Corp., 32

Texas Gas Transmission Co., 659
Thiel, R & D, 278
Third Dimension Studio, 305
Thompson-Brown Co., 384
3M Company, 948
Timber Structures, Inc., 600
Time Equities Corp., 429
Titan Fastners, 27
Titan Group, The, Inc., 254
Title Insurance Co., of Minnesota, 946
Together, Inc., 256
Torin Corp., 766
Torrid Oven, Inc., 34
Tower Mfg. Co., 777
Toyo Printing Co., 135
Transamerica Corp., 797
Travenol Laboratories, Inc., 586
Treecrop Co., The, 462
Triad Offset, Inc., 260
Triplett Corp., 746
Trojan Yacht, 823
Tropical Air Pump Mfg. Co., 105
Trust Co. Bank, 727
Tubeco Pipe Mfg. Co., 259
Turbo Train, 201
Twentieth Century Fund, The, 161
Tyler Pipe, 465
Typagraph Corp., 88
Unifair, Inc., 454
Union Planters National Bank, 647
Unit 1, 522
United Banks of Colorado, 10
United Engineers, 92
United Management Services, Inc., 641
United REfinery Co., 625
United States Air Force Documentary
    Art Program, 528
United States Air Force Systems
    Command, 762
United States Department of the
    Interior, 328
United States Leasing Realty Advisers,
    Inc., 598
United States National Park Service,
    Harper Ferry Center, 788
United States Plywood, 924
United Trust Co., 362
United Virginia Bank, 968
United Yark Products Co., Inc., 411
Unitree, 814
Universal Airlines, 208
Universal Development Corp., 635
Universal Oil Products, 811

Virginia Commonwealth University,
    258
Virginia National Bank, 608
Vision Craft Ltd., 665
Vitriform Corp., The, 763
WCIV Television, 544
WGN Television, 931
WMAL-FM, 545
WMAL-TV, 543
WPIX Television, 505
Wagner Industries, Inc., 507
Walter Kidde & Co., 223
War/Peace Report, Inc., 453
Ward Nassee Art Gallery, 688
Waring Products Division, 810
Washington Mutual Savings Bank, 714
Washington Natural Gas Co., 943
Washington Steel Co., 320
Waters Associates, 571
Watkins-Johnson Co., 440
Watson Manufacturing Co., 900
Webb & Company, 243
Weinscnel Engineering, 292
Welsh-Hannafin, Inc., 268
Weltz Ad Service, Inc., 687
Weschsler Coffee Corp., 612
Westel Co., 530
Western International Hotels, 324
Western New York Savings Bank, 655
Western Savings & Loan Assn., 841
Western Union, 723
Westinghouse, 933
Westinghouse Broadcasting Co., 503
Weyerhaeuser Corp., 469
White House Conference on Youth, 11
White Lines, 386
Jniversal Ultrasonics, Inc., 379
Uniworld Export Corp., 35
Upjohn Co., 497
Uptrend; Trend Industries, 942
Urban Systems, Inc., 837
Utica Duxbax Corp., 623
Valentine Pulp & Paper Co., 122
Vance, Sanders & Co., Inc., 427
Vaponics, 196
Vargas Zippers, 737
Varian, 199
Varo, Inc., 5
Velsicol Chemical Corp., 391
Vibrodyne, Inc., 39
View Seal, 72

White Lines, 286
Williamette Industries, Inc., 363
Shelby Williams Industries, Inc., 650
Willow Creek Apartments, 17
Erick Wilson, Inc., 603
Windecker Research, Inc., 728

Wood Electric Corp., 901
Wool Bureau, The., Inc., 630
Worcester Center, 820
World Airways, Inc., 385
World Carpets, 958
Worthen Bank & Trust Co., 949

Worthington Foods, 866
Xerox Corp., 980
Yosemite Park & Curry Co., 484
Youngstown Steel, 920
Ziegler, B.C. & Co., 964

Index of Designers

Advertising Designers, Inc. 818 N. LaBrea Avenue, Los Angeles 90038; 251, 252, 253, 254, 401, 439, 447, 457, 458, 460, 462, 264, 474, 585, 587, 589, 613, 747, 757, 758, 760, 762, 763, 764, 773, 785, 786, 915, 959, 960

Primo Angeli Graphics, 350 Pacific, San Francisco 94111; 265, 753, 754, 755, 697, 781, 808, 842

Appelbaum & Curtis, 333 E. 49 Street, New York City 10017; 27, 28, 31, 32, 104, 152, 163, 222, 224, 450, 453, 454, 456, 459, 461, 463, 759, 798, 809

Associated Advertising, 22 West Luck Avenue, Roanoke, Virginia 24001; 859, 879

Bruce Beck Design Associates, Inc. 205 W. Wacker, Chicago 60606; 16, 17, 68, 157, 975

Boatright, Bailey & Huckaba, 107 Madison Street, Memphis, Tennessee; 175, 247, 437

Jerry Braude & Associates, Designers, 8032 W. Third St., Los Angeles, 90048; 130, 190, 213, 317, 364, 452, 992

Keith Bright & Associates, 717 N. La Cienega, Los Angeles; 250, 266

David L. Burke Design Corporation, 415 N. Dearborn, Chicago 60610; 278, 279, 280, 802

Center for Advances Research in Design, 645 N. Michigan Avenue, Chicago 60611; 72, 110, 150, 174, 849, 990

Chermayeff & Geismar Associates, 830 Third Avenue, New York City 10022; 9, 10, 11, 12, 13, 14, 15, 168, 204, 209, 212, 242, 248, 262, 263, 264, 327, 328, 396, 397, 398, 422, 508, 644, 689, 690, 691, 692, 765, 766, 767, 768, 787, 788, 820, 970, 982

Cutro Associates, 47 Jewett Avenue, Tenafly, New Jersey 07670; 413, 694, 695, 696, 749, 750, 836

Dickens Design Group, 13 W. Grand Ave., Chicago 60610; 115, 145, 473, 507, 510, 511, 715, 771, 845, 850, 921, 976

Gregory Fossella Associates, Two Park Sq. Boston 02116; 65, 113, 142, 189, 192, 195, 196, 214, 277, 290, 406, 476, 654, 660, 688, 834, 883, 981, 984, 986

Fowler & More & Company, Continental National Bank Tower, Englewood, Colorado 80110; 26, 245, 249, 288, 366 431, 432, 625, 800, 804, 969

Gianninoto Associates, Inc., 133 East 54 Street, New York City 10022; 21, 233, 367, 686, 851

Philip Gips, 244 E. 58 Street, New York City 10022; 25, 176, 347

Goldsholl Associates 420 Frontage Road, Northfield, Illinois 60093; 1, 2, 53, 59, 202, 231, 300, 609, 610, 617, 620, 731, 819, 882, 888, 931

The Graphics Studio, 8721 Beverly Blvd., Los Angeles; 36, 71, 109, 135, 291, 424, 434, 658, 741, 742, 815, 817, 937, 988

Malcolm Grear Designers, 391-393 Eddy Street, Providence, Rhode Island, 02903; 29, 69, 198, 201, 218, 345, 418, 491, 605, 606, 607, 775, 780, 840, 848, 853, 985

Richard Hess Inc., 271 E. 49 Street, New York City 10017; 485, 496, 498, 499, 500, 501

Kramer, Miller, Lomden Glassman/Graphic Design, 1528 Waverly Street, Philadelphia 19146; 37, 45, 46, 47, 48, 225, 226, 227, 228, 229, 298, 373, 592, 639, 803

Lippincott & Margulies, Inc., 277 Park Ave., New York City 10017; 84, 217, 234, 423, 523, 700, 702, 778, 932, 938, 966, 967

Adrian Loos Design Studio, 2000 Stadium Way, Los Angeles 90026; 24, 62, 677, 729, 737, 839, 983

Robert K. McDonald, 2659 Knob View Rd. New Albany, Indiana, 47150; 255, 777

Alver W. Napper, Jr., 46 Johnstown Road, Albany, New York, 12203; 58, 698

Page, Arbitrio & Resen, Ltd., 595 Madison Avenue, New York City 10022; 368, 710, 843

Parkhurst & Associates, 8032 W. Third St., Los Angeles 90048; 193, 194, 267, 430, 714, 784, 842, 846, 847, 872, 873, 925

Robert Pease & Company, 1636 Bush St., San Francisco 94109; 3, 712, 824, 825, 826

Alan Peckolick Graphic Design; 118 E. 59 Street, New York City 10022; 307, 354, 429, 769

Remington Advertising, Inc., 140 Chestnut Street, Springfield, Massachusetts 01103; 139, 285

Robert Miles Runyan & Associates, 6800 Vista Del Mar, Playa del Rey, California 90291; 66, 67, 80, 83, 97, 164, 239, 241, 732, 801, 832, 967

Salesvertising Art Int., 645 Grant Street, Denver 80203; 4, 82

Selame Design, 2330 Washington Street, Newton Lower Falls, Massachusetts 02162, 143, 197, 200, 220, 240, 302, 303, 346, 348, 349, 361, 612, 675, 676, 814, 901, 906, 939, 987

G. Dean Smith, 633 Battery Street, San Francisco; 477, 478, 479, 480, 481, 482, 483, 484, 525, 527, 528, 529, 530, 531, 532, 533, 534, 535, 536, 537, 538, 539, 540, 541, 542, 543, 544, 545, 546, 547, 548, 772

Stone Associates, 101 Park Avenue, New York City 10017; 35, 105, 215, 259, 260, 419

David Strong Design Group, 30640 Pacific Highway South, Federal Way, Washington, 98002; 441, 442, 443, 444, 445, 446, 492, 493, 494

Howard York Design, 244 E. 58 Street, New York City 10022; 176, 756

Bibliography

BOOKS

Corporate Design Programs, by Olle Eksell, Reinhold Publishing Corporation, 1967

The Corporate Search for Visual Identity, by Ben Rosen, Van Nostrant Reinhold Co., 1970.

Packaging Power, by Walter P. Margulies, World Publishing Co., 1970

The Principles in the Design of Trademarks, by Carlo Vivarelli, Neue Graphik, Switzerland, 1960.

Signet/Signal/Symbol, by Walter J. Diethelm, Hastings House, 1971.

Trademarks/USA, Society of Typographic Arts, 1968.

Trademarks — A Handbook of International Designs, by Peter Wildbur, Reinhold Publishing Co., 1966

Trademarks and Symbols, by Walter Herdeg, Graphis Press, Zurich, 1948

Trademarks and Symbols of the World, by Yusako Kamekura, Litton Educational Publishing Co., 1965

MAGAZINES

The Game of the Name, Life Magazine, November 7, 1969, Volume 67, No. 19, pp. 57-62

NEWSLETTERS

Corporate Identity, published 18 times yearly, 207 E. 37 Street, New York City 10016

BOOKLETS

Reflections (3 volumes) by Leo Burnett, privately printed by the Leo Burnett Co., Chicago, 1969-70

About the Editor

David E. Carter is the designer of a number of corporate symbols, and he taught advertising and design at two universities.

He is a graduate of the University of Kentucky, and holds a master's degree in advertising from Ohio University. His articles have been published in a number of journals, including Journalism Quarterly, The Journal of Typographic Research, The Journal of Advertising Research, and Direct Marketing.

Presently Director of Advertising/Communications at Kentucky Electric Steel Company, Mr. Carter has won more than 120 awards for his creative work in advertising, and his work has been shown in many national exhibits.

His biography appears in the Second Edition of Who's Who in Advertising.